MY *AVIATION* JOURNEY

FROM A CHILDHOOD DREAM TO AN AIRLINE CAPTAIN

CAPTAIN GERARD MOFET

◆ FriesenPress

One Printers Way
Altona, MB R0G 0B0
Canada

www.friesenpress.com

ISBN
978-1-03-914840-6 (Hardcover)
978-1-03-914839-0 (Paperback)
978-1-03-914841-3 (eBook)

1. TRANSPORTATION/AVIATION/GENERAL

Distributed to the trade by The Ingram Book Company

MY AVIATION JOURNEY

TABLE OF CONTENTS

FOREWORD

Coming out of the turbulent cloud layer, in the climb through 21,000 feet, the Boeing B737 800 NG was now transitioning into the smooth air of the clear blue skies ahead of us. The solid cloud layer and the airplane's shadow disappeared below us, and I was again reminded how fast a jet airliner could travel.

"Engine anti-ice off," I called.

"Check that," my first officer, J. P., replied.

It was an early morning departure, and the radio communications with Boston Air Traffic Control Center were pretty quiet; there were very few other airplanes airborne in that sector.

I glanced at the flight instruments and engine parameters; the airplane was performing flawlessly. Then I looked out into the horizon: the view from our office was just beautiful.

We had a long day ahead of us, over eight hours of flying to Samaná, Dominican Republic, and then back to Montreal. Hurricane Irma was about to make landfall in twenty-four hours, and although we didn't have any passengers on board on this leg flying south, we were on a mission to pick up as many Canadian vacationers as possible and return them home to safety in Canada.

Then *BANG!* In the climb through 26,000 feet was a sound I had never heard in over twenty years of being a pilot. *Did we hit something? Another airplane? A weather balloon?* All these thoughts crossed my mind in a millisecond as I looked at the left wing, which seemed to be intact. The whole airplane vibrated as if gravel and rocks were hitting the fuselage and flight controls. The engine FAIL indication was on; exhaust gas temperature (EGT) gauge was in the red with excessive temperature reading; the N1 Fan speed at 0.

We had to deal with a Severe Engine Damage Drill. J. P. was pilot flying, focusing on controlling the airplane as we now only had one engine holding us up in the sky, while I was performing the memory items and checklist required to secure the damaged left engine.

"Mayday! Mayday! Engine failure request Flight Level 200 and return to Montreal," I informed Air Traffic Control, as we now vectored back to Montreal International Airport.

"Nick, we are returning to Montreal. Please inform the rest of the flight attendants." I briefed the flight director of what just happened, but he could already tell that the left engine had major damage.

What caused that engine to fail was unknown at that time. Regardless, flying the airplane and returning it back on the ground safely became our priority.

Thirty minutes later, with a single engine approach and a successful landing in Montreal, we were back on the ground.

Paycheck well-earned that day . . .

PREFACE

✈

While sitting in my condo one afternoon in early May of 2020, I decided that after so many years of wanting to write a book, there was no better time than now to share my story about a childhood dream that came true.

My Aviation Journey is my personal story about my journey to becoming an airline captain on the Airbus A330 jet airliner and all the experiences, sacrifices, and adventures it took to make this dream come true.

My intention for writing this book is to not just share my story but to also motivate the reader—to show you that no matter how big the obstacles, challenges, or the goal itself, anything can be possible; it all depends on you. There is no magic formula for success or special skills required to achieve success or to make something come true—it just takes following some basic principles.

My story is intended to inspire, guide, and inform, while sharing my knowledge and experiences with anyone who wishes to become an airline pilot. I want to help pilots advance in their career, as well as help those who enjoy flying recreationally and have an interest in aviation.

I also believe this book will motivate anyone who has goals to make their dreams come true. Nothing is impossible in life. Whether your desire is to someday fly airplanes, become an astronaut, a Navy

SEAL, a doctor, a hockey player, a fashion designer—whatever it may be—the power to succeed lies within you.

To pursue something in life, you must first have a dream, a goal. To achieve that dream, you must see yourself doing what you desire and work hard, never losing sight of your goal. But most importantly, you must never quit.

I didn't know about these fundamental principles growing up or while I was pursuing my dream of becoming a pilot, but through my own experiences and journey, I realized this mindset, which I had all along, was what helped me to succeed. The same could happen to anyone who sticks to these basic principles.

This book is about my story: immigrating to Canada; chasing a dream to become a pilot; my time in flight school; searching for my first job in aviation; becoming a captain on one of the biggest airplanes Airbus has built; making a career as a pilot, an instructor, and examiner for a major airline; and all the adventures in between.

The lessons, experiences, suggestions, recommendations, and information shared in this book are my own and do not reflect the opinions of any airline, company or individual. My memories are imperfect, but I am sharing to the best of my knowledge.

I am excited to share my story with you.

CHAPTER 1

✈

EARLY CHALLENGES

Moving to a new country is a huge cultural and environmental change for any ten-year-old kid to go through. Not only that, but I left all my friends, changed schools, and moved to a new home. Everything new and unknown made for an interesting experience.

While in university in Moscow, my mom had an engineer friend that was invited to Montreal for the Expo 67. Upon his return, he showed her some pictures of the city and told her that people spoke French there. She always loved the French culture and was intrigued by the pictures. My mom knew she would move to this place someday— and she did on November 8, 1985.

My dream of becoming a pilot had started at a very young age. My parents traveled often when I was growing up, and being in an airplane had always been exciting for me. I was eight years old when I first had the opportunity to visit the cockpit on a British Airways flight to Europe. Walking into the cockpit that day has been a lifelong memory for me, and it feels like it only happened yesterday. The cockpit was huge, with switches everywhere, and I was in awe. The pilots looked like superheroes to me with their white shirts and stripe bars on their shoulders. Right there and then, I knew that I wanted to be just like them when I grew up.

In 1975, I was born in Nahariya, the northernmost coastal city of Israel, and grew up in one of the oldest cities in the world: Jerusalem. My childhood bedroom was filled, from wall to wall, with pictures and posters of airplanes. Many times, I would find myself lying in bed, staring at those airplanes, imagining what it would be like to fly them.

I have great memories of growing up in Jerusalem. As kids, we spent most of our time outdoors, playing sports and riding our bikes. I think we spent more time outside than in our own homes. We often went on many school trips, which allowed us to see the country and discover beautiful places. Jerusalem is like no other place in the world—the diversity of religions and cultures is just amazing. School was also very advanced; at the age of ten, just before leaving for Canada, I had already started learning Arabic and English in school.

My love and passion for airplanes started in an unusual way. I was ten years old and found myself staring at a desk clock. On the background of the clock was a world map, and the second hand had a little airplane suspended on it. As the second hand was rotating clockwise, the little airplane was spinning around the world as well. At that moment, I was imagining myself inside that little airplane, flying around the world. That was when I looked at my mom and told her that no matter what happened in the future, I would be a pilot one day. To this day, I believe my decision was made at that moment.

Before we moved to Canada, my father flew there a few months earlier to help set up a place for us to live and with hopes of finding employment. My mom, twelve-year-old sister, two-year-old brother, and I would join my father six months later. Each of us kids could take one backpack on the flight, and we desperately tried to fit as many toys, books, and kid stuff in that bag as possible. Everything else we had to leave behind. My backpack was so full that the zippers stretched to their maximum limit before tearing apart.

There we were, off to a new country, leaving our schoolmates, school, neighbors, friends, and family behind and embarking on a journey and long transatlantic flight to Montreal.

Today, in my forties and looking back, I think about the courage, sacrifices, and hard work my parents had to undertake so that we could move to Canada. My parents are immigrants who made two big moves in their lives: moving from Russia to Israel in the early seventies, and then from Israel to Canada in the eighties. I am proud and forever grateful for all they have done for us. I can only imagine how tough it must have been for them to move to a new country where they didn't speak the language and had no family or friends around, no employment guaranteed, and just the unknown up ahead.

My father became friends with a Greek man who offered to help find an apartment for us to live in once we arrived. Since the apartment wasn't ready yet, we had to sleep at Mirabel Airport the first night we arrived in Montreal. The next day, we moved to a small four-story hotel located on Parc Avenue in Montreal, near Mount Royal.

The first night at the hotel, I awoke to my mom's screaming. Fire and smoke were coming up from the floor beneath us, and the only way out of the room was from our fourth-story window. We were all standing by the window, my baby brother in my mom's arms, as we watched the firemen maneuvering the fire truck ladder towards our window. We had to get out of the burning building fast, but the ladder was just not long enough to reach our room. My mom, who barely spoke English at that time, started screaming, "Three children! Three children!" in a desperate attempt to get some help.

I felt as if we were in a movie and my whole family had an acting role in it. Surprisingly, I wasn't scared. Was it because I was ten and didn't know what fear was at that time? Or maybe I just felt that everything would be ok.

We didn't have much time and had to get out of the room as soon as possible. My father grabbed the three of us in his arms, and when he opened the room door, we saw the whole hallway was engulfed in white smoke. My mom and dad, with the three of us in his arms, started running to find the nearest exit. The smoke was dense and thick, blocking any normal breathing. I couldn't see anything as thick white smoke continued to fill up the hallway. At this moment, I knew we were in trouble and started to get very nervous. I'm not sure how my father managed to see anything, but he got us out of the burning building and saved our lives.

When I think about it today, looking back, when there is a fire, people usually run away and try to exit a burning building, but firemen walk the opposite way—into the flames—which is one of the most unnatural things to do for any human being. These are the real heroes. This fire incident was a big early lesson for me. No matter how bad and dangerous the situation is, there is a solution to the problem. I learned from my dad: he made a decision and bravely dealt with it, never for a second giving up.

The next day, we moved into a one-bedroom apartment on Wiseman Avenue, near Jean-Talon Street. Three kids and two parents in a tiny little 400-square-foot apartment. Winter was approaching fast, a huge climate change from the country we moved from.

It was almost December and I still hadn't been accepted to school yet. To keep myself busy, since I didn't have much entertainment such as games or a TV, I came up with the idea to remove the ice that had accumulated around the window frames with a butter knife. It wasn't very interesting, but it kept me busy until the day a letter had arrived from the school board. A spot had opened at the St. Simon Aporte Primary School. I was so happy that I jumped up and down on the bed. Although it seemed forever waiting for a spot in school, I learned the value of patience and staying optimistic early in life.

We stood in front of our apartment on my first day of school, waiting for the school bus to pick me up. As the bus was approaching, I could see that it was packed with kids jumping and moving all around. In all my life, I had never seen a big yellow bus, never mind one picking up kids and bringing them to school and then returning them home at the end of the day. In Israel, my sister and I walked miles every day to and from school; therefore, this seemed strange and scary at the same time.

I thought to myself that maybe the parents of all these kids in the bus had given them away and now my turn had also come. I thought maybe it was too hard for my parents to have all of us at the apartment, and they had no choice to give us away. *Would I ever see my sister or baby brother again?*

I kissed my mom and up I went onto the bus. There were kids everywhere from different cultures, races, colors, height, and ages. Everything was new to me, and I had never seen such diversity. Not to forget, I didn't speak a word of French, nor English. All I had in my hand was a piece of paper that my mom gave me to show to anyone that spoke to me. I walked down the bus aisle until I found an empty seat, which was next to a blond girl that was about the same age as me. She asked me something, but of course I didn't understand a word she said and just showed her the paper in my hand, which had my name and the class I was supposed to be in. The only words I knew in French or English at that point in my life were "ok" and "Coca-Cola."

Once arrived at the school, I managed to find my teacher, who took me to the class and introduced me to the other students. It was a school for new immigrants, and although I couldn't communicate with anyone yet, I didn't feel like I stood out from anyone—at least physically.

The good thing is that kids learn a new language quickly, and since I was assigned to a French-speaking class and immersed in that environment, I was able to speak the language comfortably within six months. This experience was a big lesson for me early on that I had to work hard and learn a new language as quickly as possible if I planned on making new friends and not playing alone during school recess.

In the following school year, instead of taking a school bus, I walked thirty minutes each way to school, rain or shine. On the way back home, I would pick up empty pop cans and beer bottles and bring them to the grocery store for a refund of five cents apiece. By doing this, I was able to make one dollar on average per day, which was a great way to self-supplement myself with candies and chocolate. I can say that this was my first lesson in earning money. I learned that if I wanted something in life—which at that time was candy and later in life becoming a pilot—then I just had to work hard for it.

Another school lesson that helped me later in my aviation career was when I forgot to hand in a project on time. At the end of the school day, the teacher asked everyone to hand in their project. Unfortunately, in my case I forgot the project at home. I left a note to my teacher and ran home to get my paper, then ran back to school to hand it in. I had been so stressed for forgetting the project and worried I would get a bad grade in that class. That taught me a lesson to be responsible and organized, which helped me throughout my career.

Picking up empty cans and the desire to work led me to my first job at the age of thirteen—delivering newspapers—which was my introduction to responsibilities and a work schedule. Most kids at that age spent time playing video games, but instead I decided my time had to be productive.

Also at that age, I started reading about airplanes, theory of flight, and aerodynamics. I was curious about airplanes and wanted to know everything about how they operated, their design, and how they flew. Often after school, I would spend countless hours at the public library. At that time, YouTube did not exist; therefore, books were the tool to learn and get information.

ICE HOCKEY

I fell in love with hockey as soon as we arrived in Canada and couldn't wait to get on the ice and join the rest of the kids in my neighborhood.

The first pair of skates that I got were a speed skating model that my mom bought for $2.50 at a thrift shop. The skates were old with rusty blades, but I didn't care; I couldn't wait to get on the ice.

At that time, we lived on Decarie Boulevard, near Cote-Vertu metro station. The neighborhood was a long stretch of apartment blocks with mostly immigrant families.

There was an ice rink in a huge park behind our apartment block, and I couldn't wait to try my skates. But as soon as I stepped on the ice, I flipped over, landed on my butt, and hit my head. I had no idea how to skate or what I was supposed to do with my legs to move forward. I hurt myself badly but got up again, or should I say, got up to my knees and slowly put one blade on the ice to get the feel of what I was doing. I practiced every day, and after about a week, I felt comfortable on the ice.

We eventually moved again to a new neighborhood where I met Oren, who invited me to play hockey with his friends. We played hockey almost every day, and that was one of the best times of my childhood. We spent all the free time we had playing hockey outside; once it got too dark or freezing out, we would continue playing hockey in Oren's basement with his brothers. We eventually organized our team with Oren's younger brother and some of our neighborhood friends. All we did was play hockey and had a blast doing it.

One day I took the position of goalie since the player who held that position in the team couldn't play anymore. From that moment on, I knew that was the only position I wanted to play; there was something about stopping hockey pucks with your body. I enjoyed the responsibilities of keeping a net free of pucks, the technical aspect of goaltending, the pressure, and the encouragement from my teammates when awesome saves were made.

We used to take old sofas thrown in the trash, remove the cushions, and make goalie pads from the foam. I used a baseball glove, and the rest of the goalie gear was handmade from whatever I could purchase in a used sports store.

I eventually signed up to play in a hockey league and had the opportunity to play in some tournaments. I took hockey very seriously and made sure I progressed and learned all the time.

I played well and learned the sport quickly but not without practice. I studied the sport, and I had good reflexes and was able to read plays well. Being athletic and fearless from having pucks flying my way was a bonus. Goalies have something in common: to never give up trying to stop the puck. And never giving up was a mindset I carried later in life and in my flying career.

My goalie idol was Patrick Roy, who at the time played for the Montreal Canadiens. I studied his game and learned his style of play.

Every summer, I worked to save money for the next season, since hockey was an expensive sport to play and especially for a goalie. I got a job cleaning a sports bar, where my morning tasks included sweeping, mopping the floors, vacuuming the pool tables, cleaning the restrooms, loading up the fridges with soft drinks, and whatever else needed to be done. I was paid $15 for a couple of hours of work, and I worked every day, besides weekends.

A team I was playing for during one particular year had gone to a high-level hockey tournament. We weren't the favorites to win, but we played well and I was able to make key saves, which allowed our team to get further into the tournament.

We were eliminated in the finals, and at the end of the game, we were given tournament medals. Our team captain, Steve, had received the MVP medal, which was given to only one player. Once the medal was put around his neck, he skated over to me and put it around mine as we all stood on center ice. "You deserve it, buddy," he said as all the parents and spectators of the game clapped and cheered. That was one of the highlights of my hockey memories.

As I was advancing in hockey and going up in levels, getting around to hockey games and practices was becoming challenging. At seventeen, I was trying for a midget-level hockey team, where many other goalies were also present in the tryouts. Most goalies there had spent the previous summer in hockey school to be ready for this stage. I couldn't afford to go to such a school, since they were very expensive, but despite that I was determined to do well in the tryouts and not let the high competition get to me. The only downside to joining the team was that I would have to miss a lot of school days, as the season required lots of traveling, commitment to practices, and games.

I had to decide at that time if I was to pursue hockey and give up on school, which could prevent me from becoming a pilot someday. I realized that I would need a lot of financial support and help to continue hockey that season and couldn't ask my mom to sacrifice everything for me while my brother and sister also needed her attention and help.

After a lot of thinking and consideration, I sadly decided that I needed to leave hockey and focus on school. Although hockey was a big part of my life and I wanted to advance in it, I had no choice but to let it go. I eventually withdrew from the tryouts and decided to sell all my hockey gear. The monetary value versus what my goalie gear meant to me had no comparison. The day I sold my hockey gear was one of the saddest days of my life. I felt as if a part of me was taken away, and it took me a long time to get used to not playing hockey anymore.

As a personal belief, I think despite the very few that make it to the NHL (National Hockey League), it is possible to reach that level with a lot of hard work, dedication, and lots of support.

On a positive note, thirteen years after those tryouts, at the age of thirty I had the chance to play hockey again. I just completed my last flight of the day, and once I arrived at home base, I was told that the chief pilot wanted to see me.

As I was walking to his office, I wondered to myself if I had done something wrong.

"Gerry, do you have anything planned tonight?" he asked when I entered.

"No, boss, nothing special, just heading home," I replied.

"Good, then you are coming with me!"

"Where are we going?" I asked slightly confused

"Just bring your credit card."

We drove to a store that sold used sports equipment, and I still was confused about what we were doing there.

"I put aside a complete set of hockey goalie gear for you. Now that you are making good money, you're going to join my hockey league and start playing hockey again."

Dave knew that I played high-level hockey before and wanted me to play again and join his airline pilot league.

Although it had been thirteen years since I last skated, my skills at playing hockey came back very fast; playing goalie was in my blood. Of course, I wasn't as flexible nor as fast as I used to be, but I was back at it within minutes. It was amazing, and it felt so good to be back on the ice. After that year, again I took a break from hockey, as I moved between provinces through my career. However, I did start playing hockey again in a league at the age of forty-two and still play to this day.

For me, on the ice is the most relaxing and stress-free place I can be. A great feeling passes over me, one where all my worries and thoughts disappear, and the only thought on my mind is to enjoy the moment. My only focus is the puck, having fun, and enjoying my time with the people I play with. I am a competitive person and playing in a beer league satisfies this need. I hope to keep playing as long as my body will allow me to.

I hope that every young child who loves the sport and wants to make a career playing professional hockey, or any other sport, should go all the way. I learned a lot playing hockey; the sport taught me a lot about life, and I used those valuable lessons in my aviation career. Hockey taught me discipline, hard work, focus, dedication, how to work individually and on a team, and to never give up.

2020 vs. 1991.

HOW AVIATION ALL STARTED FOR ME

I was eleven years old when I saw the movie *Top Gun*, with Tom Cruise, for the first time. It was 1986, and I was in summer camp. My group and I were sitting on the floor watching the movie on a little TV hung up on the wall.

Seeing the first few seconds of the movie—with the exciting music soundtrack playing, the cool shots of the airplane carrier, and the F14 Tomcat—was an unbelievable moment. I knew this movie was not like any other movie I have ever seen before.

Tom Cruise's character made it just so cool to be a pilot. The character was so courageous, confident, and an excellent pilot, and his go-getter, everything-is-possible attitude appealed to me. I was probably not the only one who felt this way after watching the movie, and I am sure that military recruitment for pilots increased after the movie's release.

High school was overall a good experience for me; I was often involved in many sports. Going to airshows in the summer was something I did often, and building airplane models was my favorite pastime. Summers were dedicated to working to save money for the hockey season and, when I turned fifteen, for my first car. My goal was to purchase the Honda CRX Si, which at that time was a very cool sports car to have. I learned early on, while I was picking up cans and bottles to buy candy, that everything is achievable in life, and if buying my dream car was my goal, then I would have to stay on target and work hard until I made it happen.

I was working at the Orange Julep when I was fifteen, which is a fast-food restaurant shaped like an orange in Montreal. During my lunch breaks, I would head over to the Honda dealership showroom, sit in my dream car, and imagine what it would be like to own one. Sometimes dreaming about something can feel like the dream is a reality, which makes the goal more achievable.

The year after that, I got a full-time job in the summer working as a stock clerk at Toys "R" Us and then moved to part-time while going to school. I saved every single penny from my paycheck. Just before turning seventeen, I purchased a used 1990 black Honda CRX and couldn't be happier. What an amazing feeling of freedom and accomplishment to turn seventeen and buy your first car. Now I could drive and did not have to take the bus and metro anymore. I owned and enjoyed the car for nearly twelve years without having any mechanical troubles, besides some basic maintenance. Thank you, Honda!

Dreaming about owing my first sports car and then finally purchasing it taught me and proved again to myself that no matter what your life situation is, you can achieve anything!

My 1990 Honda CRX si

AFTER HIGH SCHOOL

I grew up in Saint-Laurent, a suburb in Montreal close to the Montreal-Dorval Airport. Near my neighborhood was the Canadair airplane factory that manufactured the CRJ jet and the water bombers CL215 and 415. The factory was built right on Cartierville Airport, which had a single runway with taxiways leading to the factory's hangars. On some occasions, even the F18 fighter jet would frequent that airport. I used to spend hours in the park next to this airport, watching airplanes land and take off.

After high school, I continued my education at Dawson College in downtown Montreal, in an engineering program. That wasn't my first choice, but back in '94, a pilot's license would cost on average $6000 Canadian, which I didn't have. I figured I would study in a field somehow related to aviation.

I did a lot of research regarding a way I would be able to finance flying lessons, but the only other option was a loan from the bank requiring a co-signer. My mom would have had to co-sign the loan, but I didn't want her to take the risk. I'm not sure we would have qualified anyway.

In the early nineties, the Internet wasn't as easily accessible or available as it is today; therefore, searching for flight schools or loan programs was very difficult. Now with the technological advancements of today and all the apps and accessible information, it is much easier to do so than my time after graduating high school.

The downfall of studying downtown and in a field I didn't find very interesting was the temptation to skip class and spend more time in the mall across the street from the college. I would go into a bookstore and read about airplanes and look at air force magazines. I would then head to my car, listen to Rush's "Roll the Bones" album on my CD player, and think of how I could become a pilot and make that goal come true.

I believe education is the most important period for people as they grow up and go through the schooling system. But it is important to study something you are passionate about and know you want to do as a career. Going to school just for the sake of going, I think, is the wrong approach. With today's information so easily available to everyone, there should be no reason to enroll in a school or program you have no interest in pursuing or spend valuable time and money in the wrong program.

One afternoon between classes, I decided to go and visit the Canadian Air Force recruiting office not far from the college. I wanted to see if there were any openings and opportunities to enter a pilot program in the Air Force. The military always intrigued me, and I saw myself making a career in the military.

I showed up at the recruitment center early Monday morning. I opened a huge wooden door and walked in. My excitement began to build. I had to continue down a long narrow hallway before I found a recruiting officer sitting at its end. I approached the desk with a big smile on my face.

"Hello, are you here to sign up to become a pilot?"

"Of course, sir, it has always been my dream to become a pilot and no better place than in the military," I replied.

Unfortunately, I did not meet the requirements to apply, therefore I had to look at other options to start my flight training. Sometimes our first choice does not materialize; that wasn't the first time, and won't be the last, a door closed on me when I pursued a flying opportunity, but it pushed me even more to continue the quest to making my dream come true.

"When one door closes, another opens!"

— *Alexander Graham Bell*

WHAT WERE MY OPTIONS?

Once the first semester of college came to an end, I decided not to sign up for another semester. I had no interest in the program I was enrolled in. Instead, I decided to join my high school friend for a two-week trip to Europe and Israel. I needed a break from dead-end jobs and school as well. I needed time off from years of studying and working, with hopes that the trip would recharge me and create a new path once I returned.

We planned to stay for a week with friends in Belgium, and then the second week in Israel. We enjoyed our time in Europe, and once in Israel I had the opportunity to visit family, do lots of sightseeing, and, of course, enjoy the nightlife.

What was supposed to be a week stay in Israel ended up being two months. Twice I had to extend my return ticket to Canada. Since I needed spending money for that extended vacation, my mom had to sell some of my personal belongings back home and send me the funds.

I eventually returned home to Canada during the middle of the winter. The vacation and travel recharged me; I felt good and motivated. But it was hard during the first few days of my return to get used to the cold weather again, as I had just spent a couple of months in a warm climate. Nevertheless, I was well-rested and determined to find a way to start flying lessons.

I had one big problem, though—I was broke! So broke, in fact, that I couldn't even put gas in my car. I needed a job badly. I borrowed my mom's car and started driving around the city looking for any work I could find.

After handing out many résumés at various stores and factories on my drive home, I stopped at an office supply store that had a huge "Hiring" sign in the parking lot.

I walked into the store and filled in a job application form. The store was empty, as shelves were just being installed. The starting pay was low, but it didn't matter at that time; I needed work and the start date was in a couple of days, which was great.

I got the call a few days later and was hired as a stock clerk. Despite the pay being low and the job itself not interesting, what made the job bearable were the friendships I made and the people I got to work with. Peter, Jimmy, Sergio, and I become very close, as we were all almost the same age, had a lot in common, and joked and fooled around all the time. Despite what was going on in our lives, we were having fun. Sergio had the same dream of becoming an airline pilot. We talked about airplanes all the time and what it would be like to be an airline pilot and fly all over the world. We even used to have our lunch breaks outside in the store's parking lot so that we could watch airplanes on approach to Runway 24R of the Montreal-Dorval Airport.

In the nineties, whoever wanted to take flying lessons or become an airline pilot had few options to choose from as far as a flight program. The first step was to get your Private Pilot License (PPL), which at that time cost close to $6000 Canadian. This pilot license allows the holder to fly as a pilot or co-pilot of an airplane and to have passengers on board recreationally as well. This is the most held license in Canada and is the first license earned by an aspiring professional pilot. A pilot without this license cannot work.

The next step is the Commercial Pilot License (CPL), which allows the holder to fly professionally as a pilot of a single pilot airplane, or as a co-pilot on a multi-crew airplane. The CPL includes more advanced piloting knowledge, skill, and experience than the PPL. Commercial pilot training is the requirement of earning an Airline Transport Pilot

License (ATPL). Lastly, you will need a multi-engine rating, which will enable a pilot to fly a twin-engine airplane, and an instrument rating, which a pilot must have to fly under instrument flight rules (IFR).

In the late nineties, all these qualifications would have cost an average of $25,000 to $30,000 depending on the school or flight club, the hourly rates schools charge for instructors, and the airplane rental. Today, in 2021, for the same licenses the cost of these programs has almost doubled, to an average of $60,000 if done in a flight club and more than $90,000 on average if enrolled in a college program.

During the time I was working at the office supply store, researching about flight schools wasn't as simple as it is today, thanks to the abundance of information available on the Internet. In my time, the Internet wasn't readily available, which made research very difficult, and there was a lack of guidance on how to pursue a career as a pilot. Even with the Internet, though, there isn't much guidance out there for want-to-be pilots, which motivated me to write this book—I made a commitment in my profession to help and guide future pilots in their quest at becoming airline pilots.

My first option was to save money and take flying lessons as I continued working at the store, but that would have taken a long time to complete the private license. Moreover, flying lessons need to occur regularly to enable a good learning progression, which does not happen with big gaps between flights. But unfortunately, my paychecks weren't high enough to afford the flying lessons, and I didn't have any money saved up; I was just twenty.

My second option was a bank loan, which, as I said before, required my mom to be the co-signer of, and I was not certain we would even qualify for one.

The last option was a flight college, which often had a student loan or bursaries programs, but unfortunately I wasn't aware of one at that time until the day Sergio came to work with some exciting news.

He told me about an open house for a private flight college located near the Saint-Hubert Airport, in a city near Montreal, which would be held in a week. The name of the college was CESPA (College Enseignement Superieur de Pilotes d'Aeronefs), and it offered student loans for a complete pilot training program, which included a Private Pilot License, Commercial License, and the multi-engine and instrument rating. I was ecstatic about the news and couldn't wait for the week to go by.

CHAPTER 2

✈

A GOLDEN OPPORTUNITY

The first thing I noticed when arriving at the school was that everything about it was new and modern, from the building itself to the classrooms. The second thing was that there were plenty of visitors at that open house; there were probably close to 300 interested in the flight program that day.

After a short tour of the establishment and a brief question-and-answer period, we were invited to complete an aptitude and basic academic knowledge entry exam, which lasted approximately thirty minutes. Once completed, we were told that those selected would be contacted soon with more information about the application process.

Sergio decided not long after the college visit to pursue an aircraft engineering program in another college in Saint-Hubert and to get his private pilot courses from a flight club instead. Aircraft maintenance has always been a high-demand profession, with lots of opportunities after graduation.

I was accepted into the pilot program, which also enabled me to graduate with a college diploma in aviation studies. But there was one condition I had to meet: I had to obtain high-level math and physics credits from another college, as I was missing those credentials to enroll in the program.

I also met with the chief flight instructor as part of the acceptance process into the program. During my interview, he asked if I was certain and aware of the big student loan that I was about to sign. My answer to that was, "Where do I sign?"

He smiled, and then with a serious face, he asked me again, "There are not going to be many or perhaps any jobs out there once you graduate in two years. Have you spoken to your parents about the student loan and are you aware of all responsibilities and conditions related to the reimbursement?"

The student loan was for $65,000 to cover the whole two-year program, which included a diploma, a PPL, a CPL, a multi-engine and instrument rating, and an average of 220 flight hours on the following airplanes: Cessna 152/172, Katana DA20, and Piper PA-44 Seminole twin. The loan was co-signed by the Government Ministry of Education and would have to be reimbursed after graduation.

It was important for the school that the applicants were aware of the big student loan involved with this program and of the challenges present in the industry at the time. That was winter 1997, when the industry had hardly any pilot job opportunities, especially for new graduates. Major airlines were even laying off pilots.

I was aware of the commitment I was undertaking and the challenges I would face after graduating, but I had been waiting for this opportunity for a very long time and couldn't wait to start school.

In my gut I knew this was a once-in-a-lifetime opportunity, and if I was going to pursue my dream, CESPA was the golden opportunity— the ticket to becoming an airline pilot.

AVIATION COLLEGE

I started flight school at CESPA in March of '97, and it was an exciting moment for me. Finally, I was going to study the thing I was so passionate about. It felt like I was fulfilling a purpose and a goal.

In that college, student pilots had the choice to enroll in French-speaking or English-speaking courses. Since I am fluent in both, I decided to enroll in the English section for the following reasons: Firstly, most aircraft manuals are written in English; therefore, learning all the technical terms in English would make it easier to understand those manuals. Also, English is the language most used in aviation and in Air Traffic Control communication; therefore, learning the lingo is very important for a student pilot right from the beginning.

Including me, there were only four students in the English section who started that March semester, whereas in the French section there were over twenty-five. Being in a small group was an advantage since we were able to get more attention and time from our teachers. Also being a small unit, we became good friends, and if one was lagging or getting ahead, then it was easier to help each other so that we all were at the same level of progression.

The first course in the program was Theory of Flight, which was given by a retired Canadian Air Force pilot. I was impressed with his knowledge but mostly with the way he delivered that information to us. He was a master of the subject, was clear when he spoke, and kept the course interesting, keeping everyone in the class attentive to him. It was a skill and talent I took note of in case one day I instructed. Also, the fact that we had a fighter pilot as a teacher made the school experience even cooler.

Reading many books in my late teens about this subject gave me the basic knowledge in advance and prepared me for the first enrolled courses for that college program.

The program was full-time, with activities seven days a week. We had classes every morning, lasting sometimes until midafternoon or late afternoon. The schedule varied a lot, which enabled us to take our flying lessons sometimes in the early mornings or after school. Weekends were days we also did a lot of flying. Each student had the freedom to book their flights with the instructor of their choice.

Since my acceptance to the flight college was conditional on completing two college-level courses in math and physics, I had to enroll in night classes at Dawson College for three months, the same college I was previously enrolled in for the engineering program. Classes were three days a week from 6:00 to 8:00 p.m.

Attending both colleges required good time management and organizational skills. My days would end up being very long, and waking up at 6:00 a.m. became the norm, as driving to Saint-Hubert would take almost an hour. Classes at flight college would often start at 8:00 a.m., with flight lessons in the afternoon, and then I would head downtown for a 6:00 p.m. night class.

I had exams at Dawson College almost every couple of weeks. Since I had to put priority on my flying sessions and aviation courses, I wasn't left with much time to prepare for my math and physics exams. Therefore, on some exams I would score 80% or higher, but on others below 50%. The twenty-four hours in a single day was sometimes just not enough to allow me to review all the material for my math and physics classes. Despite the stressful situation and the pressure I put on myself, I had to come up with a plan—I knew I would not be able to continue in the flight college if I didn't pass those two courses.

In the end, what I did was improve the way I was taking notes in class so that reviewing exam material would be easier. Instead of reading long manuals, all I needed to do was review my notes, but they had to be clean and clear. Also, I pre-booked many of my flying lessons on the weekends so that during the week I was able to dedicate more time to studying.

I eventually passed these two courses, with a mid-sixties average in both. Although I always strived to aim for high grades, I was just happy to pass and to finally meet all the credentials required by the flight college. It felt good having all that pressure and weight off my shoulders. Now I could just focus on my flying.

FIRST FLIGHTS AND EARLY LESSONS

Since I was a young boy, I would dream and fascinate about flying airplanes. How were these heavy and big pieces of machinery able to stay up in the air and fly so fast? How would it feel to handle such a marvel of equipment in the air? What does it take to be a pilot? Where are these schools to learn how to fly? Do you need special skills? These were a few of the many questions I had, and I needed to find answers.

I found many of the answers to these questions in aviation books. I would spend hours researching and reading. By doing that, I started to have a clear picture of airplane aerodynamics and what made them fly and how to control them. Building airplane models was my favorite pastime, and attending airshows was a way to meet pilots and an opportunity to ask all the questions I couldn't find answers to in books. Also, airshows are just so cool to visit.

My first flight as a student pilot with an instructor was on June 12, 1997, on the Cessna 152, registration C-GBYZ. The 152 model was a perfect airplane for an initial pilot training. The sessions started with a demonstration of the pre-flight walk-around, which is a clockwise walk around the aircraft to ensure the structure, equipment, and everything looks good. Then we moved on to engine start and taxi exercises and an hour of airborne flight time. This was it—the day I'd been waiting a long time for. I was very curious to see if everything I imagined flying to be was true. There was only one way to find out.

Once airborne, we made some basic flight maneuvers and turns, climbs, and descents, adjusting different power settings and reviewing basic flight instruments. It was an amazing feeling being up in the sky and seeing the world from above.

The connection between human and machine is a special feeling. A pilot challenges gravity by using power from the engine and lift from the wings, using flight controls to change the direction of the airplane. This brings the feeling of freedom and complete control at the same time. The cockpit became my new home.

We were planning to return to Saint-Hubert Airport, and my instructor was going over how we would join the visual circuit pattern to the airport, the landing techniques, power management, and the flaps configuration on approach.

I knew that landing an airplane would be more challenging than taking off, so I had prepared at home by visualizing what I would do with my hands and feet during the approach and landing. This technique helped me later in my flight training and career. By visualizing something prior to performing the task, you feel that you've already done the maneuver, which makes it easier when performing it.

I was able to fly the approach and land with little input from the instructor, thanks to a very good pre-flight briefing from her. But it also helped that I understood the approach and landing are all about energy management, potential energy, and kinetic energy. Managing, feeling, and understanding this energy is crucial from the beginning of flight training. Anticipating, making inputs, and observing the results are the basics of flight; a pilot implements this pattern of thinking over and over when flying.

The first flight went very well, and I couldn't be happier or erase the smile I had on my face when I stepped out of the Cessna. I knew I'd made the right decision to pursue my dreams and study in a field I was so passionate about. That first flight gave me the confidence that I would succeed in the program, and I was so eager to learn more and for my next flight.

As the training flights progressed, new exercises and maneuvers were introduced, such as steep turns, approach to stalls, recovery from spiral dives, and touch-and-go's. My first solo flight without my instructor was on July 21, 1997, on Cessna 152 C-GSZG. That was on my fifteenth training flight, with 15.5 total flight hours.

We were parked at the flight school apron. My instructor gave me a final word, wished me a good flight, and then exited the Cessna. I called the tower for taxi clearance and then proceeded for the active runway. As I was taxiing, I looked at the empty seat next to me and realized that, yes, this time I was going to be flying by myself—there would be no one to rely on or to correct or help me. I felt excited and a little nervous at the same time. The solo flight would require taking off, joining the circuit for one pattern, and then approach and landing. I had to be extra focused and ensure everything I did was well performed.

That was the first time I had to maintain altitude, speed, and navigation while also staying focused on the radio communications, being aware of the airplane traffic flying in the circuit pattern at the same time as me.

My mom came to the airport that day to see me go on my first solo flight. It felt like when she used to come to the arenas to see me play hockey; it was a nice feeling knowing she was on the ground watching me in the air.

After landing, I taxied back to the school airport apron, shut the engine down, and completed all checklists. My instructor approached the airplane with a smile and congratulated me. That was followed by a water splash from my schoolmates— a tradition after a pilot's first solo flight.

Post first solo flight, July 1997.

In aviation, like in many other professions, a student pilot will go through many steps and challenges through their progression and then later in their career. Pilots will go through many exams, flight tests, evaluations, interviews, new aircraft type ratings, and many more hurdles faced throughout the career. Being tested and evaluated is just part of a pilot's career, and it should be a learning experience, a self-challenge to improve, an opportunity to gain new knowledge, and a step forward. Otherwise the pressure will add unnecessary stress.

Also, I learned early in flight school that knowledge is key to success and accomplishment. The more I studied, reviewed, and understood the material well before a class, a training flight, or an evaluation, the better I was able to perform and succeed. Some would spend an hour on material, while others needed three hours. Regardless of the time, the key is to master the material. Time management and prioritization were very important in school.

As the program progressed, I realized the aviation industry is very competitive and that I would have to excel. Every student was good and everyone wanted to succeed, therefore I made sure to have high expectations for myself and to keep high standards.

The academics and quality of instructing at the school were top notch, but there was one topic that wasn't covered or explained to us, which was how to find work once we graduated. What steps or avenues did we need to pursue to find employment after graduating? What companies hire pilots fresh from school? What are pilot interviews like? These were a few of the many questions that flight schools didn't really provide answers to.

But there was one big piece of information one of our teachers told us during class that stuck with me: "One of the most important things that will help you all find that first job in aviation is public relations."

I understood what he meant by that and figured it would take more than just skills, experience, flight hours, and determination. Networking and public relations would be very important and key to succeeding in this field because once we all graduated, we would all have the same flight hours, same college diploma, and same experience. What would make the difference was what each student had done and what avenues they would take to search for flying opportunities.

Therefore, one of the most important lessons I learned was that the earlier a student pilot makes friendships and contacts in the industry, the better the chances for success in finding employment. This goes to anyone, even experienced pilots. People skills are as important as flying skills in the industry.

THE WORST TIME TO HAVE A
STUDENT LOAN CANCELED

The student loan for the two-year college program was $65,000 Canadian. Every few months I would receive a check from the bank, which would total an average of $12,000 to $23,000. I would cash the check in my account, and the school would withdraw a sum of money every semester.

Approximately three months into the program, we received shocking news from the Ministry of Education. We were informed that we would not receive any more student loan checks for the program we were enrolled in and that we would have to find a way to fund the remaining semesters on our own.

The news came at the worst time, just a few months after starting flight school. At this point in the program, I had received just over $12,000; there was no way I would be able to pay for the rest of the program by myself. There weren't many options for me at the time; I either had to get the money or leave the program. This devastating news was a major disappointment for all of us, and I was worried about my future.

I wrote a letter to the Minister of Education explaining that my dream was to become a pilot and that I was lucky to be in the first quarter of an aviation program. I added that I was very grateful that the government had allowed me the opportunity to go to flight school and for co-signing my student loan and that I made a lifetime obligation to pay back my loan after graduating and asked for help and understanding.

I received an answer from the government not long after sending the letter with amazing news: the student loan would remain for those of us who started the program. I was so happy that the government reconsidered. Without that loan, I would have had to exit the program. I made myself a promise that no matter what happened after graduating, I would be responsible for this loan and would do whatever was required to pay it back to the government.

STAY ALERT TO STAY ALIVE

The private and commercial pilot training stages of the flight program progressed well for myself and my classmates, but not without a close call.

One of our classmates and his instructor were on a training flight flying the Katana DA20, a training aircraft, when they found themselves seconds away from a catastrophic head-on collision with a Cessna 172.

It was a close call. This accident has a complete report available online. *Aviation Investigation Report A98Q0029.*

This event taught me a big lesson that stayed with me for the rest of my training and in my career to date. I learned that as pilots we must always be alert and focused when operating an airplane. There is no such thing as having a bad day in the office or making errors due to the lack of situational awareness, as the result could cause major damage, accidents, and even death.

The aviation industry, although very regulated and safe, had to come a long way to get where it is today. But to maintain that level of safety in the industry, it is important to treat our profession very seriously. Regardless of whether you are a pilot in training or an experienced captain with over 10,000 hours, staying focused and remembering that complacency has no place in our line of work is paramount.

A pilot's job is being aware of and dealing with what we call "threats." Threats exist all the time and can occur in a flight beyond the influence of the pilot. Threats include, for example, dealing with adverse meteorological conditions, airports surrounded by high mountains, congested airspace, aircraft malfunctions, and errors committed by other people outside of the cockpit. But by staying alert a pilot will be able to recognize these threats and even errors and correct them by using standard procedures or other methods.

Also, know your aircraft and its limitations, respect and understand the weather, follow procedures, and always maintain situational awareness by knowing where you are and where you are heading. With all those things in mind, a pilot will be able to enjoy a fun and safe flying career.

OBTAINING MY COMMERCIAL PILOT LICENSE

To fly for "hire or reward" and work for a Commercial Air Service in Canada, it is required that a pilot hold the Commercial Pilot License (CPL).

Part of the requirement for obtaining the CPL in 1998 was to complete a 200-nautical mile flight (370 km) to any destination chosen by the student pilot. The student pilot would have their pilot's logbook certified at every destination in that cross-country flight.

With the Private Pilot License (PPL), up to this point I enjoyed many flights where I had the opportunity to bring friends and family members on city tours and cross-country flights with me and was looking forward to bringing a close friend with me on this long flight.

For my commercial long-range flight, I booked one of the school's aerobatic airplanes: the Robin R-2160, registration C-FROB. I chose that airplane not because I planned to do aerobatics but because it had a big glass cockpit canopy, which gave great visibility for a cross-country flight. Also, the cockpit was a little roomier than the Cessna 152 airplane.

Some pilots chose destination airports in Quebec or Ontario and some planned routes to the United States. I wanted to fly somewhere I hadn't been before and chose a flight to New York, with the final stop in Atlantic City.

A lot of planning was required before that flight. I had to plan the route, familiarize myself with the airspaces, fuel endurance, and fuel stops, select an airport with customs service, and so on. As a backup to my route maps, I borrowed a GPS from a classmate, a very helpful tool for navigation. All my paperwork, maps, and planning were organized and ready for the flight. My friend, who wasn't a pilot, joined me and we departed Saint-Hubert Airport on September 24, 1998.

The first leg was a short flight to Burlington Airport to clear customs before we continued heading south towards New York. The weather was good, and we were cruising at 4500 feet for most of the flight until we arrived in the New York airspace heading to Teterboro Airport.

I had never been in such busy airspace before and tried to remain calm and not overwhelmed. The New York Center air traffic controller cleared me to maintain a specific heading and altitude and instructed me not to transmit anything on the radio until he contacted me again. The airspace was full of airplanes—anywhere I looked in the sky, I saw one. In fact, one DC9 was flying so close above me that I could read "Delta".

It was exciting, but at the same time, I had to stay extra alert, focused, and attentive on the radio so as not to miss a call from Air Traffic Control. Using visual flying rules (VFR), airplanes have a very specific and narrow corridor of airspace that must always be maintained. We were able to fly a short city tour before we proceeded to Teterboro Airport for an overnight stay.

The next day, after a good night's rest, we were getting ready to head to Atlantic City. Before departure, I performed a walk-around of the aircraft and completed all checklists; the engine start went as planned. I received taxi clearance, and as I was taxiing, the controller asked me if I was familiar with the airport since I was slowly taxiing the airplane. I replied that I wasn't too familiar with the airport and requested progressive taxi instructions to help me head in the right direction to the active runway.

I learned a few good lessons that day: Always study the airport diagram and familiarize yourself with the runways and taxiways environment. Also, when receiving a taxi clearance and after reading it back, make sure you know exactly where you are and review the route on the taxi chart before moving your aircraft. Make sure the clearance is clear before starting to move. If there is any doubt in the clearance or uncertainty, ask for clarifications from the controller. If during ground maneuvering a pilot is not sure of their position or where they are going, then it is best to ask for guidance from the air traffic controllers. These lessons are especially important when flying single-pilot, as there is no co-pilot to correct or guide you. Flying is always easier in familiar airports, but it is very different in unfamiliar airports—those we fly into or out of for the first time.

A mistake pilots often make is to taxi prematurely without really knowing where they are going because they fear they will block an aircraft taxiing behind them. You should not completely neglect who's behind you—it is always important to have good situational awareness—but the priority should be on what's ahead.

Some airports—especially major international airports—have standard taxi routings from and to active runways. Therefore, it is important to review those taxi charts before starting to move the aircraft. Always make sure that crossing a runway is approved by Air Traffic Control, and if in doubt, always ask for clarification, as entering an active runway is the most dangerous thing a pilot can do—when in doubt, ask!

The rest of the flight to Atlantic City was uneventful and we landed at Bader Field Airport, Atlantic City's municipal airport, in the early evening. The airport was in uncontrolled airspace; therefore, it didn't have an operating control tower. I joined the circuit, landed on Runway 04, and parked the airplane, securing it with protection ropes before we headed to the Caesars Atlantic City hotel.

On the way to the hotel, I was going over the flight in my head—the decisions I made, the approach and landing, the things I could have done differently, and the things I learned from the flight. I found that a good practice; since everything was still fresh in my head, it was a good way to self-analyze and learn.

The next day, we left Atlantic City in the early afternoon. The flight was uneventful until the weather started to deteriorate en route, heading northbound, even though the weather was forecasted to be visual flight rules (VFR). I was observing the shapes of the clouds and analyzed my options to possibly change altitude, course, or even destinations.

I was supposed to operate in visual meteorological conditions (VMC) and with a visible horizon. Flying always had to be performed outside of clouds to maintain visual contact with aircraft traffic and with the ground. This was the first time I had to deal with weather and low clouds in flight. In this situation, I knew I needed to focus on remaining calm—the priority was to fly the airplane. I advised the air traffic controller, requesting assistance and a weather update.

To remain in VFR, I couldn't descend anymore since I had to maintain a safe minimum from obstacles below us. I prepared myself to use my instruments and to trust them no matter what and disregard any illusions that might occur flying inside clouds. Scanning the altitude indicator, then altitude/airspeed, and heading over and over would be the technique I would use to safely fly the airplane.

I was able to maintain a safe altitude and navigate the aircraft around the cloud buildup with the help of Air Traffic Control. In-cloud penetration was brief, but this was a reminder that when flying VFR and despite the pre-flight weather analysis, things can change in-flight—being ready to revert to the instruments and flying the airplane is fundamental in case of cloud penetration.

During the private pilot program, we received brief training in emergency flight solely through referencing the instruments in case all else fails and an escape from an inadvertent cloud penetration is not possible or visual reference to the ground is lost. Learning to fly this way is the most important exercise during the PPL program in my opinion. Students must master that skill early in training. There have been too many avoidable accidents that led to controlled flight into terrain (CFIT) due to loss of situational awareness.

The rest of the flight was long but uneventful. I was happy that one more step in my pilot training program was accomplished by completing the cross-country flight. We arrived at Saint-Hubert Airport late in the evening. I parked the aircraft and headed back home, thinking about the whole trip; I couldn't wait for the next step and final part of my training program: multi-engine and instrument rating.

This next stage would be my favorite part of the program, as now we would fly a bigger, more complex airplane and on instruments, which is what an airplane pilot career is based on. Also, since we were flying on instruments, we weren't relying on clear cloudless weather, which prevented us from flying the Cessna on many occasions.

The program started with a few simulator sessions. We learned how to properly scan instruments and interpret what the airplane does without using the outside horizon. We also practiced flying different types of approaches: instrument landing system (ILS), very high-frequency omni-directional range (VOR), and non-directional beacon (NDB). Using the simulator was a great tool, as many various scenarios were practiced.

After all the required simulator sessions were completed, the next step was aircraft multi-engine training, which I did on the Piper PA-44 Seminole. The Piper PA-44 Seminole is an American twin-engine light aircraft manufactured by Piper Aircraft. The PA-44 is a development of the Piper Cherokee single-engine aircraft and is primarily used for multi-engine flight training. Now I was flying an airplane with double the speed compared to the single-engine Cessna airplanes I flew before. This meant things were happening a lot faster in flight. Most importantly, this also meant I would have to accept and learn to trust and interpret the instruments correctly, understanding what they indicated and making necessary adjustments as required.

This stage of the training was the most demanding, not only because of a more complex airplane but also because instrument flight rules (IFR) are more regulated and restrictive. There are IFR clearances that

Air Traffic Control gives pilots, and the complexity of the IFR system is a lot more detailed and demanding compared to VFR flying.

Towards the end of the instrument rating stage of training, I had an important conversation with Sophie, one of our instructors. I asked her about my options once we graduate and which avenues I should pursue to look for my first pilot job. I wanted her advice and recommendations.

"Gerard, it will be challenging and very competitive to find work in Quebec. I know a past student that was able to find work in Winnipeg, on a Beech 1900 turboprop aircraft after graduation with 220 hours total time. You will have to move there if you are open to that option. Here is Pat's number. Call him after you graduate."

My Multi-engine Instrument Flight Test was completed on March 6, 1999, on the PA-44 Seminole aircraft C-GBVW, which marked the end of the flight training program and my graduation from CESPA. I completed a total of 235 flight hours with a Commercial Pilot License, and a multi-engine and instrument rating. It had been the busiest two years of my life, but what a fulfilling experience and accomplishment. I was happy with the program and ready to pursue a flying opportunity.

But where do I go from here? How do I go about finding a pilot job?

WHAT I DID AFTER AVIATION COLLEGE

After graduating, I was focused on starting my career and finding a job as a pilot as soon as possible. I wanted to remain current and not forget the flying techniques, practical skills, and knowledge I learned in school. It is important for a recently graduated pilot to continue flying and building experience so as not to become rusty, especially while not having much experience.

I figured even if I couldn't find a flying job right away, I would focus on looking for work at airports or at least in the aviation industry so that I could build relations and make contacts that would hopefully lead to a flying position. Also, because my school was full time for two years, I couldn't work, and therefore, at graduation, I was broke with a huge student loan. I had to find work ASAP!

Right after graduation, I ended up getting a job fueling airplanes and cleaning their interior at the college. Once the student and the instructor left the aircraft after a training flight, I would fuel the airplane, tow it to a parking position, and then secure it. This job only paid minimum wage and also required that I spend almost all my time outside, regardless of the weather conditions. At the end of my shift, I was exhausted and my eyes would be red and burning from the fumes after fueling the airplanes for eight hours. Not to mention, I received many mosquito bites and sunburns, as I was working in the summer.

Looking at the glass always half full, I saw this job as my first job in aviation; I was at the airport around airplanes and talking to people in my industry, which was all very positive. I knew that I had to make sacrifices, as many people do in other professions.

One day while at work, I heard about an airline based in northern Quebec that might have pilot openings. A couple of days after hearing the news, on my day off I drove the 800+ kilometers to go visit the airline. I figured the best thing was to go there and show my face, instead of just calling or sending a résumé, which might just end up in a pile with the hundreds of others.

The drive was not simple due to the terrain and the occasional fog at higher elevations. During the entire drive, I rehearsed in my head how I would present myself and what I would say.

I arrived at the airline's office before noon and introduced myself to the friendly receptionist. I explained that I was a pilot looking for a flying job and asked if it would be possible to see the chief pilot. I wore a white shirt, a black tie, and brown dress pants. She told me that he was busy at the moment but offered a seat to me in the meantime.

I sat by the reception for about two hours until I noticed the receptionist pointing me out to the chief pilot. As he approached me, I stood up, introduced myself with a smile, and extended my hand for a shake. I could tell he was a busy man, and me being there was more of a nuisance than anything else. Without a chance to talk much, he informed me that I didn't meet the minimum requirements. He only hired pilots with a minimum of 750 hours total time and co-pilots weren't paid.

I thanked him for his time, and the receptionist as well, and left the office. An eight-hour drive was waiting for me and I headed back home greatly disappointed. I figured the minimum number of hours was a way to eliminate those of us with 220 hours and no post-school flying experience. Also, not getting paid as a co-pilot? That was the first time—but not the last—I heard about such a practice by small operators. Some companies would not pay co-pilots, and many accepted these jobs. I wondered how I could possibly work for free with such a big student loan.

On the way back home to Montreal, I was pulled over for speeding. Although I was certain that I followed the speed limit driving on a one-lane highway following other cars, I couldn't talk my way out from getting that speeding ticket. What a disappointing day that was, and I was just crushed. Getting a ticket and being broke, tired from a long drive, hungry, and discouraged from the meeting with the chief pilot didn't make that day pleasant at all.

Along my route, the gas stations were not so frequent, and on the drive back, I ended up in a low-fuel situation. There was no way I could afford getting stuck on the highway. It was the first time I found myself in such a situation. I had to think fast and make a quick decision. I kept my speed at 80 kph, turned off the AC and all non-essential equipment, and made sure to keep the acceleration to a minimum until I got to the gas station. My pilot instincts were kicking in: stay calm, find a solution, and execute it.

I forced myself not to be discouraged from visiting the airline. I knew how much I wanted this career to start, and the more the doors closed on me, the more I knew that I had to stay positive and keep working hard if I wanted to succeed. That road trip and meeting with the chief pilot was the first of many similar situations that happened to me. I wondered if life was testing me to see how badly I wanted to fly. I couldn't let this get to me. The situation felt like a hockey game—I knew I couldn't give up until the game was over, and if I had the time, then I needed to work even harder.

Some of my schoolmates decided to continue and get an instructor rating after graduation, and a few were able to find fire patrol flying jobs in the summer months. Both options required more money unfortunately. Although a great way to accumulate hours, an instructor rating required close to $5000 at that time, which is almost triple the cost in 2021.

For the fire patrol job, the company required a type rating on the airplane—meaning you had to pay to be trained on the airplane you were going to work on first, which was close to $2500 of training fees. The company guaranteed the pilots 250 hours that summer.

There was another small company that I heard did not pay their co-pilots. These pilots worked for free, but in return they were able to build flight hours. Working for free was something I was against; I would have never accepted such a position, even if it was offered to me. A pilot is a professional, and not getting paid reduces the value of our career and creates precedence to other companies. I'm not sure if these practices still exist, but I hope no pilot accepts work without pay.

Paying for a type rating to work for the fire patrol company was not an option. I didn't have that sum of money at that time, nor the funds to enroll in the instructor course, although I always saw myself teaching in the future.

I did invest in buying a book that had a list of almost all the airline companies in the world. It also listed all the airplane types the companies operated, the addresses, and contacts. I used that book to send hundreds of résumés, which took lots of time and money. How many replies did I receive? None! Not a single reply from any company—probably because many others with the same low-level experience were doing the same and they received hundreds of résumés.

I decided then that I should call Patrick in Winnipeg and talk to him about his company and his career path after flight school. I was running out of ideas and was desperate for some advice.

Our first conversation was short, but overall Pat was friendly and helpful. He told me a little about life in Winnipeg and the two airlines that hired pilots with an average of 220 hours. Both airlines had turboprop airplanes with a capacity of eighteen to twenty passengers, operating mostly from Winnipeg to the northern communities. They flew passengers and freight as well.

Now here's what impressed me: These two airlines in Winnipeg hired co-pilots with 220 hours on twin-engine turboprop airplanes, which was unheard of in Montreal or anywhere else in the country. On top of all that, they paid their co-pilots!

If I compared these airlines in Winnipeg to those in Montreal who operated the same types of airplanes, they required a minimum of 1000 hours and 500 on a twin-engine turboprop experience. Therefore, Winnipeg had amazing opportunities.

After that first phone conversation with Pat, I continued working at the college fueling airplanes, with no luck in finding any flying opportunities in Quebec. I was fed up with the mosquito bites and sunburns, sweating all day, and breathing fuel vapors. I wanted to fly and had to make a big move and decision.

I called Pat a second time a month later.

"Pat, I'm coming to Winnipeg!"

CHAPTER 3

✈

HEADING WEST AND TAKING THE
ROAD LESS TRAVELED

The decision to leave for Winnipeg and find my luck there was because many pilot graduates were competing for very few available pilot positions in Montreal. Understandably, most preferred staying in the big city than moving somewhere far.

In my case, I decided to take the risk, or at least give it a shot, and see what Winnipeg had to offer instead of staying and probably not finding any work. Taking the road less traveled is what I had to do, leaving me to embark on this 2250-kilometer road trip. But I had never been west of Toronto before and didn't know much about Winnipeg, besides what Pat had told me and the information I was able to research.

I packed the Honda with the basics: my flight bag, some clothing, including one pair of brown dress pants, a white business shirt, and a black tie, which I would wear to meet each airline, and my electric Brother word processor typewriter.

My plan was basic: take the Trans-Canada Highway heading west and stop at every single airport along the way. Once I arrived at each airport, I would type my résumé using my typewriter, and address it to the company I was going to see. I figured this was much better than sending résumés not knowing where they were ending up.

The typewriter I carried with me to Winnipeg; I still have it twenty-three years later.

All I had with me was the $250 my mom gave me for the trip. I brought with me a Mexican blanket since I was planning to sleep in my car while on the road to Winnipeg. If I would end up finding a flying job along the way, I would make that city home; otherwise, the destination was Winnipeg.

Before I left, my mom and I just stood there with tears in our eyes. I felt bad leaving my family behind, but I had no choice. In life, we need to give to get, and this was my sacrifice. As I was pulling away from home, I could see my mom in the rear-view mirror, waving goodbye and crying.

I had mixed emotions. It was the first time I was leaving for another city and didn't know what was waiting for me. I was going to a city I'd never been to before and starting a journey into the unknown with only one goal—find a way to become an airline pilot. Desperate times called for desperate measures!

I made a list of all the airports I would be passing along my route from Montreal to Winnipeg. Once arriving at each airport, I would pull off the road and head to any aviation company in that location. I would then find a place, whether a restaurant, library, or gas station, where I could plug in the typewriter and type a cover letter addressed specifically to each company. Then I would print them, attach the letter to my résumé, which I printed before heading on the road, and put everything in an eight-by-eleven-inch envelope.

I would then change in my car, putting on my white shirt, black tie, and brown dress pants, before heading to each airline company's office with the hopes of meeting the chief pilot or any company employee to whom I could present myself and hand my résumé. I was a salesman on the road selling a product—the product was me.

At the first airport, there were two small airlines but neither had openings for a pilot position. I thanked them, asked if I could leave my résumé, and headed back to my car. I changed back to my T-shirt and jeans and continued driving to the next airport.

At the next airports along the route, I received the same responses: "We have nothing at this time," "You don't have enough experience for our requirements," "You need to already have a type rating on our aircraft," or "Just leave your résumé here and we will give it to HR." I would always ask to see the chief pilot, as I figured he or she was the one involved in the hiring, but they weren't always available to talk.

No matter the rejection from the companies I saw, I had to stay on target and not get discouraged because you never know—maybe after 1000 no's, there'd finally be a yes.

I arrived at Toronto on the morning of the second day of driving and headed to Toronto Island Airport (YTZ), now called Billy Bishop after the top Canadian flying ace of the First World War. I'd been to the city many times before and had flown to the airport during my flight school program. It was a good place to stop since there were many aviation companies.

I parked my car on Eireann Quay Street, which was quiet at that time in 1999, as airlines weren't operating from there yet. Again, I changed into my professional attire, took my flight bag with me, and headed to catch the short ferry ride to the island airport.

Walking on Airport Road, I was looking for any company I could leave my résumé with. The first place I walked into was a flight school, but I was told they were only hiring instructors. There were a couple more small airline operators, but the offices were closed.

I continued my search until I noticed an airline office building with a large hangar next to it. As I looked through the fence surrounding it, I could see small and big airplanes parked on the airline's ramp, which to me meant it was a big company and a good door to knock on.

Next to the hangar, I saw a door that I figured was the entrance to the company's offices. I knocked on it, but there was no reply. I waited a few minutes and knocked harder, but again, no one came to the door, so I waited, hoping someone would come out or walk in.

About fifteen minutes later, the door opened and a man who seemed to be a mechanic looked at me, surprised.

"Can I help you?" he asked.

"Hello, sir, my name is Gerard. Would I be able to speak with the chief pilot if he is available?"

"Just wait here inside the hangar."

I followed him into the hangar and sat on my flight bag after the mechanic disappeared into a small office. I waited in the hangar for about forty-five minutes when suddenly I heard someone shout at me.

"Hello, come on up here." A man dressed in shirt and tie waved at me to come upstairs before he turned around and walked back in his office.

As I looked up to the hangar stairs leading to the second floor, I figured that was where the airline's Flight Operations offices were.

I found a way to get to the second floor, introduced myself to the man, and thanked him for taking the time to see me.

"How can I help, young man?"

"I recently graduated from flight college, and I'm on the road, driving out west from Montreal, looking for a flying job," I replied.

"Unfortunately, the minimum flight experience required for a first-officer position with us is one thousand hours and jet or turboprop flight hours. I suggest you head up north; that's where the jobs are to build hours."

The one thousand hours minimum kept coming back almost every time I spoke with a company for any flying opportunities. I was just wondering how the other pilots managed to get those hours if no one out there was hiring us after school. Perhaps he was right, most of these hour-building jobs were up north in the remote areas.

"Thank you, sir, for your time and recommendation. I am heading to Winnipeg to see if there are any opportunities there. Would I be able to leave my résumé with you just in case anything opens up in your company, or perhaps you would be able to forward my résumé to any of your contacts?" I asked.

He took my CV, got up, and headed to the back of his office. I wasn't sure where he was going, but I figured maybe to photocopy my résumé. A few minutes later he returned, but this time he didn't have my résumé but a small piece of paper in his hand.

"That's for you," he said.

Initially, I thought it was a business card, but when I took the paper and unfolded it, I saw it was a check for $115. I wasn't sure whether that check was for me or given to me by mistake.

"Is the check for me?" I asked, a little confused.

"May I ask where you are staying while on the road to Winnipeg?" the man replied.

Embarrassed, I answered, "I'm on a tight budget. I'm sleeping in my car to save money for gas and food until I get to Winnipeg."

"You look horrible and you stink. A shower and a good night's sleep will do you good. Deposit this check and get yourself a hotel room before you hit the road," the man replied.

I shook his hand, thanked him for everything, and left his office back through the hangar. As I was walking back to the ferry, I started crying like I hadn't cried in a long time. I cried not only because of my struggles and difficulties but because of what had just happened. I would say these were tears of joy. For the first time since graduating, and after all the job searching, this man gave me hope. This $115 check felt like my first pay in aviation and a reward for my work. I felt this man believed in me and encouraged me that it was going to work out in the end.

I got into my car and headed to Toronto Pearson Airport to see if there were any companies I could give my résumé to.

After handing out some résumés, I decided it was time to get some rest for the night. I found an abandoned parking lot on the north side of the airport and decided to spend the night there. Sleeping in my car at an abandoned parking lot at Toronto Pearson Airport didn't discourage me. The jet engine noises of the departing airplanes kept me motivated. I told myself that one day I would be taking off from this airport.

I could have cashed the check the man so generously gave me, but I decided to save the money for food and gas. Despite my big Mexican blanket and this being summer, I was freezing as I slept that night in my car. I probably only slept an hour or two, waking up often to start the car and warm up.

I hit the road early the next morning, as I had a long way ahead of me. Spanning east to west across Canada, the Trans-Canada Highway is a single-lane highway with thousands of trucks on it. Passing these trucks was not a simple task, especially when a few of them were tailing each other. I'd driven on many highways in my life, but this was a very challenging road; I gained a lot of respect for truck drivers and their challenging profession. Being able to stay up for hours and driving wasn't easy, and something I hadn't done before.

After drinking all the coffee I could, listening to music, singing, and doing everything I could to stay awake while driving, ten hours on the road made my eyes grow a mind of their own and I fell asleep behind the wheel.

WELCOME TO FRIENDLY MANITOBA

Sometimes, we learn the hard way. After driving such a long distance without stopping, your eyes can play tricks on you, or at least mine did. I was an hour and a half away from Winnipeg and thought that if I pushed it a little longer, I'd be able to make it to the city. But after driving for such a long period in the dark, my eyes closed as I drove.

I don't know how long I passed out for, but I woke up to the sound of gravel and rocks hitting the underside of the car and the wheel well. I was on the shoulder of the opposite lane with a truck coming right at me!

As I grabbed the wheel and brought the car back onto the correct lane, I was in shock and couldn't believe how I had gotten into this situation. Meanwhile, the truck in front of me honked and flashed his high beams at me. This time, I pulled off the road for good and slept the night in my car. It was almost 2:00 a.m.

I woke up as the sun was rising and headed back on the road. I entered Winnipeg through Main Street and then turned left onto Broadway. I stopped at a gas station and decided to wash my car. I couldn't see through the front windshield anymore because of the thousands of dead mosquitos and bugs.

My initial thoughts about the city were that it was so small compared to Montreal, with very few high rise-buildings. But it was charming, and the people seemed very friendly and helpful. Also, the drivers seemed to be a lot calmer than the fast-paced Montreal and Toronto drivers. I felt like I was in a more relaxed and easy-going city.

I called Patrick, and he invited me to come over to his place, which wasn't very far from where I had stopped. It was nice to finally meet him and his girlfriend, Dominique; they were both very friendly and hospitable. They offered to let me stay with them for a week while I visited the airlines and looked for a place to live, which I was very grateful for. After four days on the road, I was very happy to finally sleep horizontally in a bed and not in a Honda.

I woke up early the next day and got ready to go see Pat's airline. The great thing about Winnipeg is that everything is close by, and the road system is simple.

I walked into the office and was greeted by Jenn, who was a pilot but working in the office, which was one of the many different positions pilots held, I'd soon find out, as they were waiting to get on the line with the airline. I introduced myself and talked a little with her. She then offered me a seat and told me to wait for her chief pilot, who would be arriving to work soon.

I sat not far from Jenn and looked around the office, thinking about the road I'd been on to get here, the people I'd met and the events along the way, and that I was finally here in Winnipeg. Maybe this was going to be my lucky day? Who knew? I was happy I was there and was looking forward to meeting the chief pilot.

The chief pilot walked into the office, and I could hear Jenn telling him about me, that I was from Montreal and looking for work as a pilot.

As he walked towards me and as I got up to say hello, he said, "You are blocking the board."

I was sitting in front of a whiteboard he needed to use. I changed seats, figuring he was too busy to talk to me; I didn't want to bother him.

He stood in front of the board for a few minutes and did some writing. From what I could tell, he was looking at the pilots' schedule. Then he turned around and left the office. I was confused and disappointed at the same time; I wasn't sure why he wouldn't take a minute to talk to me. In my search for work during the last few months, I had met several busy chief pilots who couldn't talk to me for more than a minute, but this was a different situation. Maybe he was just having a bad day.

Disappointed and sad, I thanked Jenn for her help and asked if I could leave my résumé with her. As I was just about to get into my car, I saw Jenn wave to me from the office.

"Are you interested in working as a cargo loadmaster? The chief pilot just called me."

"Of course, that will be great," I replied.

"Be back on the other side of the airport at the cargo location tomorrow at 10:00 a.m."

"I'll be there at 10:00 a.m. sharp. Thanks, Jenn." I didn't know anything about the position but was glad I had found work.

For the rest of the day, I went grocery shopping. I was surprised to hear so many French-speaking people at the grocery store. Their accent was very different, though; it didn't sound completely French-Canadian, it had a mix with anglophone. It reminded me of home, and at that moment I felt homesick and missed my family. But I had to stay positive. I was happy that at least I had a job waiting for me the next day, which would allow me to start looking for a place to live.

I arrived at the airport the next day at 9:30 a.m. and proceeded straight to the cargo office. I wore my usual white shirt, black tie, and brown pants—the only business attire I had—as I figured I would probably be interviewed for the position and therefore wanted to be ready. I had even brought my flight bag with some résumés in it.

I walked into the office and was told to go up to the second floor, where I found the pilots I was assigned to work with and introduced myself. Both pilots were sitting by a desk, going over some paperwork. I cannot say that they were the friendliest guys I had ever met. We didn't talk much; they told me that there was a cargo aircraft on the ramp that needed to be loaded and to go find the load master, who was already on the ramp.

There was no talk about where we were flying to or anything about the job, no employment forms to fill, pay, or anything at all—just, "Go on to the ramp and start loading the airplane."

I headed first to the bathroom to change from my shirt and tie. Luckily, I had a white T-shirt on underneath; otherwise I would have been loading an airplane with a shirt and tie and that would have looked weird.

It was a hot, boiling summer day. Those who think Winnipeg is a frozen, cold city are partially right: it does get unbelievably cold during the winter months, but the summer can also get very hot—and this was one of those hot days.

I went outside and was met with another pilot who was working the ramp. There was a lot of cargo on pallets and barrels that needed to be loaded onto the aircraft, and after a couple of hours, we managed to put everything on board.

The pilots came out to the ramp, and I headed up to the cockpit, where I joined them sitting on the jump seat. I was pretty much drenched in sweat and exhausted at this point from loading all that cargo.

The pilots were not able to start engine number one on the aircraft, and after a few attempts, the captain called a mechanic to come out and investigate. As the mechanic arrived, he went up on a ladder, opened the engine cowling, did some looking around, and topped up the engine oil. While he was doing that, the captain looked back at me and said, "Did you know that if one of those engines quit in flight, we'd be dead?"

Maybe he wanted to show that he had a sense of humor, but that wasn't funny at all.

The mechanic went back up on the ladder and told the captain through the cockpit window that the engine needed work and that the airplane was a no-go! The captain then looked at me and ordered that I unload all the cargo and come back tomorrow at the same time.

After unloading all the cargo, I headed to the parking lot and sat in my car, exhausted and disappointed. I decided to call the other cargo loader I had met that day on the ramp.

I asked him how many pilots were working on the ramp and about the time frame it took for flying positions to open. He told me that about ten to twelve pilots were working the ramp at various positions, waiting to get on the line. On average, there were one or two flying openings every four to six months. I did the math and figured my time on the ramp would be very long—at least a couple of years before I would see any flying opportunities!

I had to reconsider coming back the next day. The dilemma I found myself in was that with this non-flying position, I wouldn't be flying for a few years, and while waiting for my turn at such a slow pace, I could risk missing opportunities with other companies. Even though I had known many pilots who'd started their careers by taking ramp positions and working their way up to a flying spot, I also knew there were risks to it: besides potentially missing opportunities elsewhere with other airlines, I could get injured on the job, as most positions were physical and in dangerous environments, and lose valuable time. I headed back to Patrick's house discouraged from my day.

After some thinking, I decided to call the airline and pass on the cargo loader position.

The following day, I was on my way to Winnipeg International Airport to visit Perimeter Aviation, an airline that had its separate passenger terminal on Ferry Road, on the southeast side of the airport.

I walked into the terminal, approached the check-in counter, and asked one of the agents if I could speak with the chief pilot. She offered me a seat in the passenger lounge and said she'd see if she could get a hold of him.

I grabbed a seat next to a table that had a coffee machine on it and waited. Not long after, the chief pilot showed up and introduced himself. We headed out to the parking lot for a brief chat. He was very friendly, and I enjoyed talking to him. We talked for about five minutes and just before he left, he said, "Gerry, you seem like a nice guy with a head on your shoulders. I was just hired with a regional carrier and will be leaving Perimeter soon, but you should come by again in about a month and see the new chief pilot, Mark, once he is all settled in."

I thanked him for his time and was happy for the opportunity to speak to him. I had a good feeling in my heart after my visit to Perimeter and saw this as a positive first step. This was the airline I would pursue.

All I had to do was count down the thirty days before my visit to see the new chief pilot.

NEED TO PAY RENT

Waiting a month was a long time, but as the previous chief pilot suggested, I had to give Mark time to get settled in his new position. In the meantime, I had to look for any work I could find to afford a place to live. I had no more money left and couldn't stay with Pat.

I started looking for work in malls and at big retail stores. I also drove down major streets and handed out résumés to various companies. One day, while job searching, I came upon a big gym. From the outside it looked very fancy, and with the number of cars in the parking lot, I figured it was a popular place to work out.

I had been lifting weights since I was thirteen and had been going to gyms in Montreal all my adult life. I figured why not go to this gym and see if they would have any job openings.

I walked into the gym and met the manager. She explained that they had an opening to work the front desk, sell memberships, and assist the members. I replied that I could do all of that and asked if I could start right away. I got the job!

The pay was minimum wage, and the shifts were twelve hours long, four days a week, but there was a commission for memberships sold. I was very happy—I was working in a clean environment, could work out for free at an amazing gym, and my coworkers were very cool. I found making new friends easy at a gym, which was good since I didn't know anyone in the city besides Pat and his girlfriend. The only negative part about working there was the constant pressure from the manager to sell memberships, and she wasn't very nice when I wasn't able to close a deal.

Working at the gym kept me busy, and staying fit felt great. The money was enough for rent and food, but nothing else besides that. I was late by two months on my rent because it took time to get my first pay, but it wasn't enough to pay the past rent I had missed. The property manager, and eventually the owner, began to constantly harass me to pay up. I had one credit card and it was maxed out.

My meals consisted mainly of Kraft dinner and vegetables and, on occasion, tuna cans; in fact, Kraft dinner was on the menu almost every day. The one-bedroom apartment I lived in was empty, with no furniture besides an inflatable mattress and two plastic milk crates that I used as chairs.

I'm not sure if that classified me as poor, but I didn't have much as far as possessions or money—I had a car, some clothes, and that was it. With the temperature below -35°C almost daily, winters in Winnipeg were very cold, but I had to cut down on heating the apartment, as I couldn't afford the high electric bill. There was an association in the city that helped poor people; they gave used clothing and other goods for those in need. They gave me bus tickets, which I sold to one of the janitors at the gym to make a little extra money.

One day my work colleague gave me a used TV as a gift, which I was so happy to receive. It still had the rabbit ears and I could only receive two or three channels. But regardless, it was great, and I was able to watch some shows and *Hockey Night in Canada* in the evening after work.

In 1999, the membership at the gym was considered expensive and not everyone who walked in for a tour of the facility would sign up right away. Every membership I sold gave me a commission, which was helpful, but I just couldn't pressure visitors to get a membership.

At one time, a pretty girl entered the gym, and I gave her a tour of the fitness center. She liked the gym, but once we went over the membership plans, she said she couldn't afford it. There was nothing I could do if the person just couldn't afford the membership.

"What happened there?" my boss asked after the girl left.

"I showed her the gym, and she was impressed with the equipment and classes, but once we went over the membership options, she said that she needed more time to think about it," I replied.

"No excuses, Gerry. Do whatever it takes to sell, even if you need to ask the girl out."

I'm not kidding—that was what she said.

On my days off, I would often drive to the airport and park my car behind Perimeter's terminal. I would sit there for hours and watch Perimeter's Metro II airplanes taxi in and out of the apron. I knew this was the airline I would work for. My time working at the gym and my financial difficulties didn't discourage me but instead made me more eager and hopeful to find my first job in aviation. I was still counting down the days to see Mark, but I was worried about how our meeting would go. What would I do if it did not go well?

EFFORTS EQUAL RESULTS

A month had gone by since my first visit to Perimeter, and it was time to go back and hopefully meet the new chief pilot. I wore my usual: white shirt, black tie, and brown pants.

Now that I'd already been to the airline's terminal, I knew exactly where to go. I walked in and went straight to the check-in counter and asked the agent if I would be able to see Mark.

"He hasn't walked in yet, but he usually walks through this main passenger entrance," replied the agent.

"That's perfect, thank you. I'll just grab a seat by the entrance. If I miss him, would you kindly let him know that I would like to introduce myself and take a couple of minutes of his time?"

"You bet," she replied.

I took a seat right next to the entrance to the terminal to keep an eye open for the chief pilot. After meeting many of them before during my job search, I knew what to look for and I made sure not to miss him. Chief pilots are busy people. They usually walk fast, holding a cell phone to the ear, so missing them could be easy and I did not want to miss this opportunity.

A couple of hours later, I spotted Mark walking into the passenger terminal and heading straight to the table with the coffee machine on it. He wasn't wearing a pilot uniform when he came in, but as the ticket agent had described him, I figured that was him.

I got up and walked quickly over to him as he poured himself a cup of coffee. As I walked towards him, I went over what I was going to say in my head, which I had practiced for a month, so that I didn't lose his attention. This was it!

Mark had spiky blond hair, clear blue eyes, and a goatee; he was medium built. He made direct and piercing eye contact, had a serious composure, which was intimidating, and seemed like he had a busy day ahead of him, so I chose my words wisely.

"Hi, Mark, it is a pleasure meeting you and congrats on your new position. My name is Gerry and I recently moved to Winnipeg from Montreal. Are there by any chance open pilot positions at your airline?"

"Nice to meet you as well, Gerry, and thank you! I need to head to my office, but you can come with me. We'll chat there."

Once in Mark's office, I had a chance to explain that I had recently settled in Winnipeg and had met with the previous chief pilot. I told him that I would love to have the opportunity to work for his airline and asked if he would be able to review my résumé. Mark asked me a few questions about my aviation goals and why I wanted to work for Perimeter.

"Generally, we hire instructors from Perimeter's flight school, pilots that are currently working on the ramp, and, on occasion, pilots from the outside. There are many pilots currently applying, but there are no openings now. But I'll keep your résumé on file."

"Thank you, Mark, for your time. I appreciate it, and it was nice to talk to you. My dream is to work for your airline!" I shook his hand, handed him a copy of my résumé, and left his office.

I left Mark's office knowing that it would be very competitive and not easy to get on with this airline. I figured many pilots were applying, which was understandable. It seemed like a great company to work for and an amazing flying experience on a high-performance airplane.

On a positive note, I had the opportunity to meet Mark, and we had the longest conversation I had had with a chief pilot to date. In some way, it was a small interview.

I decided that no matter how long or how difficult it would be, I would work for Perimeter; it was my top choice. I knew I was putting all my eggs in one basket, but patience brings rewards!

After meeting Mark for the first time, I kept going back to Perimeter, on average, every two weeks, either on a Monday or a Tuesday, depending on my work schedule at the gym. I wore the same clothes each time I went to see Mark: my white shirt, black tie, and brown pants. I figured by wearing the same clothes he will not mix me up with other applicants in case there were many others doing the same. Why every two weeks? I didn't want Mark to forget about me, and I knew it would show my determination and that I was still available to work for his airline. I knew I was competing with hundreds of others who also wanted to work for him, so I thought this would make me stand out from the crowd. At least, I felt I was doing something positive.

My routine was to walk into the Perimeter passenger lounge at 7:00 a.m. and sit next to the coffee machine. I knew from the first time I had met Mark that the coffee table was his first stop before heading to his office. Why did I go on a Monday or Tuesday? I figured that at the beginning of the week, a chief pilot would probably have meetings, and therefore, I would have a chance to see him.

He would usually walk in to work between 7:30 and 8:00 a.m. Sometimes, he would come to the coffee machine, pour himself a cup of coffee, and after being surprised to see me there, would make one of the following comments:

"Gerry, what the hell are you doing here?"

"Gerry, what happened? You sleep here again?"

"Gerry, weren't you here a couple weeks ago?"

Other times, he would walk straight to Dispatch and wave at me. Sometimes, I would sit there by the coffee machine and Mark would not work on that day. By doing this every two weeks, I figured it was not often enough for Mark—or any other airline employee—to get angry at seeing me there, but also not so infrequently that he'd forget about me.

Was I desperate? Yes, I was!

Besides being a way to show my effort, dedication, and desire to work for Perimeter Aviation, I figured it was my only option at that time. All I did was show my face and express my interest without disturbing or annoying anyone. Would I recommend doing that today? That depends on the shape the industry is in. Many airlines would probably be against this practice. When the industry is in good shape, sending résumés or having someone inside the company bring one to HR will probably result in an interview, but when things are slow, résumés are just going to end up in a pile.

But this was 1999, and these were different times in aviation. The industry was slow; there were many pilots without work, and major airlines were not hiring. These were competitive times, and I had to do anything and everything I could to get that first job in aviation, which at times seemed impossible without any experience or contacts.

"Effort equals results."

I believed in this quote and in my strategy. I had to remain positive, focused, and keep myself occupied. I had come a long way and my mission was to join Perimeter.

SOME GREAT NEWS

In September, three months after I met Mark for the first time, he invited me to a Metro II aircraft ground school that was given by the company's operation's manager. The ground school course reviewed many technical aspects of the airplane and procedures. It was scheduled for three full days and took place at Perimeter's conference room. The ground school course was given to newly hired pilots and currently employed pilots as a refresher.

Mark told me that I was not being hired but was welcome to sit in the ground school. I was extremely happy to be given the opportunity. Now, was this a sign that I would eventually get hired? Who knows? But it was for sure positive, and although I didn't want to get my hopes too high, I was overall super excited.

I managed to get hold of an old Metro II airplane flight crew operating manual (FCOM) to review and familiarize myself with the airplane as much as I could before the course. At that time, I was not sure how many pilot openings were available, but many pilots were taking the course that morning. The ops manager, who was giving the course, was himself a captain on the Metro aircraft and was extremely knowledgeable of the aircraft's systems and very technical. It seemed like he designed the airplane; that was how detailed the course was.

The Metro II is a pressurized, twin-engine turboprop aircraft limited to a maximum takeoff weight of 12,500 pounds (5,670 kg). Powered by the powerful and efficient Garrett TPE331 turboprop engines, it is classified as a "high performance" airplane because, by the Canadian regulations, it requires a minimum crew of one pilot and has a never exceed speed (VNE) of 250 knots or greater, or a stalling speed or the minimum steady flight speed in the landing configuration (VS0) of 80 knots or greater. Passenger seating capacity is up to nineteen. Advanced training was also given to captains, as the airplane was operated into short northern gravel runways.

Swearingen Fairchild Metroliner SA227

Swearingen Fairchild Metro II SA226 cockpit.

Once the ground school finished on the first day, I headed home to review the day's material. I put all the manuals and my notes on the kitchen counter and reviewed everything that was explained in the course that day. I was told to expect a question period the next day, where the ops manager would pose a question or two to each person in the course, so I had to know my material well.

The question period began that next morning. When my turn came, I didn't answer the first question precisely and the ops manager corrected me. Disappointed at myself, I made sure to take better notes that day and be better prepared for the next question period.

I went back home, had dinner, and was up until 1:00 a.m. reviewing all the material. The next day, I answered all three questions well.

After ground school, I continued working at the gym and kept myself as busy as I could. I reviewed the course material on occasion and kept seeing Mark every couple of weeks on average. The winter was approaching, and the weather was changing fast.

I knew Winnipeg was a cold city in the winter but was shocked one day to see on the weather channel that the outside temperature was -52°C with the wind chill. I looked out of my apartment window, and everything was icy cold outside. I wondered to myself if it was even safe to step outside in such temperatures.

As I left the apartment for work that day, approaching my car, I noticed that most of the cars in the parking lot had an electrical cord extending out from the engine compartment, which was plugged into an electrical port. It was the first time I had seen something like that and thought to myself, *Are these cars electrical?* I tried starting my car, but of course, with the temperatures that day, the Honda didn't want anything to do with that; it was frozen stiff.

All the other cars had a block heater, which is used in cold climates to keep the engine oil warm to start the car. I needed to get one urgently if I wanted to have a car that winter. I had no choice but to take the bus to work that day, which required a lot of walking in the cold.

The winter of 2000 was very cold in Winnipeg. It was hard being away from family and living in almost poor conditions. Four months had passed since the ground school at Perimeter, and some days were hard, while other days I kept my spirits high. Working out and socializing with people at the gym helped me a lot.

During this time, my older sister, Catherine, who lived in Montreal, gave me courage and motivated me. She had encouraged me from the beginning of flight school and while I was in Winnipeg waiting to get hired by the airline. She told me that the sacrifices I made would pay back one day. Often, she would ship me a box full of my favorite chocolates and candies to keep my spirits high.

Although we were far apart and I couldn't visit my family often, they were with me in spirit all the time. Succeeding in aviation wasn't just a personal goal, but also for my family. I wanted to show my little brother, by example, that with hard work dreams will come true.

PILOT LICENSE NOT VALID

Around this time, I was contacted by a licensing agent from the Aviation Authorities, who informed me that my Commercial Pilot License was not valid and that I would need to retake my Commercial Pilot Flight Test. I was surprised and thought it must have been a mistake since I had passed the Commercial Flight Test successfully in May of '98. I was told that since the school did not send the required paperwork on time for my license application, it was not valid and I would need to redo the test portion.

I called the school right away to get more clarification, but nothing could be done. It was a paperwork mistake, and I had no choice but to redo the flight test. I was in shock and couldn't believe that this was happening. First, I hadn't flown for almost a year; I wasn't prepared for a flight test. Also, since I had to be recommended to do the test, I needed to fly with an instructor, which would involve renting an airplane and spending money I didn't have. This couldn't have happened at a worse time; I was stuck in a very bad situation. My landlord wouldn't be happy, but my rent money would have to be used to cover this situation.

I had no choice. I had to do the flight test; otherwise, I would not have a valid license and couldn't be employed by any airline. I prepared myself as much as I could and booked a training flight at a flight school in St. Andrews Airport, located north of Winnipeg.

Despite the bad timing and this unfortunate situation, it was nice to be back in the air and to fly an airplane again. I missed flying so much. I was recommended and successfully passed the flight test.

CHAPTER 4

✈

2000—A NEW YEAR AND NEW BEGINNINGS

It had been over two weeks since I last visited Perimeter, and it was time to go back again to say hi to Mark. I woke up as usual that Tuesday morning at 6:00 a.m. It was dark out and a typical cold, freezing day. I was waiting for my white shirt to dry while I ate a small breakfast. Shirt and pants ironed, black tie on, and shoes shined, I was off to the airport to arrive before 7:00 a.m.

I walked into the passenger's lounge and, as usual, sat next to the coffee machine to keep my eye open for Mark. For some reason that day I was tired; I hadn't slept well the night before. An hour after I'd arrived, Mark walked in and headed to the coffee machine.

I got up. "Good morning, Mark, don't want to bother you. Just came to say hi."

"What are you doing here, up so early?" Mark replied.

"Ah, well, just wanted to say hi and tell you that I can't wait to work for Perimeter so that you don't forget about me."

I was just about to say thanks and leave when Mark replied, "Gerry, grab a cup of coffee."

I grabbed a Styrofoam cup, poured myself a black coffee, and followed him to his office. As we were walking, I thought to myself, *This is it; he's going to tell me to stop bugging him, that there are no open positions, and he'll keep my résumé on file.* My thoughts were racing through my head.

"So, Gerry, how's everything going at work in the gym?"

"It's good, Mark, not selling as many memberships as my boss would like me to sell, but I'm doing my best on every shift."

"Look, Gerry, no one has done what you've been doing. Everyone sends their résumés and calls, but you are the only one who's been coming here all the time. That's a lot of dedication on your part, and you deserve it. You deserve the next first officer position. You are the next first officer on the Metro II that I am hiring!"

This was one of the happiest days of my life and certainly the highlight of my pilot career. I was so happy, the words didn't sink in. I graduated flight school in March of '99, almost a year earlier—it had been a long road to get to that special day.

Every effort equals a result—which I had proven again that day. After so many rejections and times where it had felt as if nothing was going my way, I finally arrived at this special day and a new opportunity.

Mark said that I would be called soon with my start date. The hiring process would first consist of simulator sessions to freshen me up on instrument flight rules; then three training flights with Mark on the Metro II—which would total approximately five hours—would follow. After that, I would take a Pilot Proficiency Check (PPC) Flight Test with the ops manager, who was also the company's check pilot. Once that was all done, I would take line indoctrination training on revenue flights, and once I completed that, I would release as a first officer (FO) and pass the training program.

I thanked Mark, shook his hand, and told him how happy I was and that I looked forward to the training. That was January 25, 2000—a date I will never forget.

I went home to hit the books, reviewing my IFR and reading the Perimeter SOPs and all my ground school notes. I gave the gym my two weeks' resignation notice. No more selling gym memberships. I was going to fly airplanes!

TRAINING ON THE METRO II

My first simulator session was on February 26 at the Perimeter flight school. The sessions lasted two hours and overall went well, despite it having been a year since my last IFR flight.

Two days later, I had my first training flight with Mark on the Metro II aircraft registration C-GIQG. I met with Mark in his office, and we went over the weather, Notice to Airmen (NOTAMS), and the plan of the training flight. We then headed out to the ramp for the aircraft walk-around.

After our engine start, we headed to an open ramp area next to the threshold of Runway 31 to perform some aircraft systems checks and avionics setup prior to departure. After that, we taxied to the active runway and proceeded for takeoff. The acceleration was well pronounced since the airplane was empty, and even without using full takeoff power, the acceleration and rotation speed (VR) happened quick. The airplane felt heavy on the control column during rotation, but once the nose gear was off the ground, it leaped into the air. Once airborne, and after initial contact with Departure Control, we received some radar vectors and then were cleared to intercept the airway northeast.

For those who have not flown the Metro II, it is a unique airplane when it comes to handling and is not simple at first. It's an airplane that needs to be well trimmed for it to fly well and for you to be able to do anything else. If the airplane is not well trimmed, you won't be able to maintain altitude and focusing on any instrument approach or tracking an airway will not be possible. The airplane does not have a functioning autopilot.

The control column on the aircraft has a couple of switches that are used to move the trimmable horizontal stabilizer. A horizontal stabilizer is used to maintain the aircraft in longitudinal balance, or trim. Initially, I was using too much trim, which caused the airplane to oscillate and prevented me from maintaining the exact altitude. I had to relax and use trim at small increments to maintain altitude. By holding the control wheel with just a few fingers, I was able to "feel" if the airplane was trimmed or not. Holding the control wheel with a tight grip prevents a pilot from getting a good response from the flight controls.

I was behind the airplane and could tell Mark was unimpressed with my performance. But I managed to grasp the airplane trimming and was able to focus on other tasks. Next, we entered the block of airspace reserved for us to do some upper air work, which included steep turns, approach to initial stall and recovery, and a few other exercises.

We then descended towards St. Andrews Airport, a small regional airport north of Winnipeg, and entered the holding-pattern exercise. I had learned the theory for this exercise in aviation college, but in operation it was quite different. The speeds the Metro was traveling at reduced the time available to make decisions or figure the hold entry procedure compared to the slow-moving school airplanes I was used to.

After a couple of turns in the hold, we proceeded to do the non-directional (radio) beacon (NDB) approach, followed by a circling approach. A circling approach is the visual phase of an instrument approach to bring an aircraft into position for landing on a runway that is not suitably located for a straight-in approach. On our approach that day, we arrived at 1,500 feet east of the airport and then circled on the west side to line up with Runway 36—all while maintaining altitude and a minimum speed of 140 knots and staying within 1.7 miles of the airport. On top of that, I had to keep all the other small Cessna aircraft that were in the circuit pattern in sight. It was busy!

We cancelled the approach at Minimum Descent Altitude (MDA), and I flew the missed approach procedure. We then proceeded back to Winnipeg to fly the Instrument Landing System (ILS) approach for a full stop landing. The approach went ok, and as for the landing, I had some coaching from Mark with the power management. The Metro is a numbers airplane, meaning specific speeds had to be maintained on the approach, and I eventually had to memorize the torque setting to maintain during approach.

After landing, Mark taxied the airplane to Perimeter's parking area and shut the engines down. The airborne part of the flight lasted an hour and twelve minutes, and it had felt like it was a marathon. As we were putting the engine covers on and securing the aircraft, I replayed the whole flight in my head. I was not fast enough with the procedures, although I studied hard. Things were happening very fast in our airspace. St. Andrews' airspace was busy, with many airplanes airborne at the same time and frequent, distracting ATC communications.

I hadn't flown a twin engine airplane for almost a year, and the last twin I'd flown wasn't even close to the performance of the Metro. The airplane was fast and needed precise handling. I was also not familiar with Winnipeg's airspace and procedures, which didn't make things easier during the flight.

On a positive note, after that first flight, I learned how to handle the beast and understood the trimming techniques. Now that I'd been to St. Andrews and flew the approach there, I knew what to expect and in general was more familiar with the pattern of the training flight. I understood what I had to focus my studies on.

As we were walking to Mark's office to debrief, I was picturing what he would tell me about the training flight and knew it would not be good.

"Gerry, this is too much for you. I'm not sure you will make it," he said.

I was crushed. I was so grateful he had given me this opportunity, but there I was—below the standards. I took notes of every detail and comment in Mark's debrief of the flight. I could tell by his comments that two more training flights would not be sufficient to be recommended for the flight test.

"Mark, I was not up to standard, but I know now what I need to work on. It's been a while since I last flew, but I will work hard and will be ready to do much better on the next flight. Give me the chance. I will not let you down!"

I felt down, drained, and disappointed in myself. I was worried that I might fail the training and not be able to make a career as a pilot. It had been a long road, and I couldn't believe that this was the situation I was finding myself in. But I wasn't defeated yet. I knew what I had to work on, and I knew what to expect on the next flight.

The next day, I went to the Perimeter hangar, found a Metro not being worked on by the mechanics, and did what is called "hangar flying." I sat in the airplane and studied, reviewing the memory items and all the drills, touching all the switches, and memorizing where they were and how they felt. I went over the whole training flight right there in the cockpit—there is no better classroom. I spent hours hangar flying, and my confidence was growing.

I had another simulator session. I was able to practice what we had done on our first flight, and although it was a simple twin engine simulator and not a Metro, I was still able to have a good learning experience, especially when it came to instrument approaches. I had one more simulator session on March 2 and felt a lot more confident. I had time to go over all the exercises and approaches I would be expected to fly on the next training flight.

Right after the second sim session on March 2, I was on my way to meet Mark in his office for the second training flight. It had been three days since the first training flight, and I was a lot more comfortable and ready for this one. I had to put the pressure aside, knowing that if I didn't do well, I might lose the opportunity to fly for Perimeter. A training flight is not a test—therefore learning is key!

Mark had very high standards and didn't allow much room for error. I looked up to him and learned a lot from him and his style of flying and approach to being a pilot. "Good is not good enough"—that was how Mark saw things.

The second flight was far from perfect, but much better than the first flight. The third flight went well, and Mark recommended me for the test flight. I had 5.2 hours of training, including night touch-and-go landings.

The test flight was on March 6 on aircraft C-GPCL, and I was officially type-rated Metroliner II (SW3) designator on my license. I was hired at Perimeter Aviation as a first officer on the Metro and finally got my first job as a pilot.

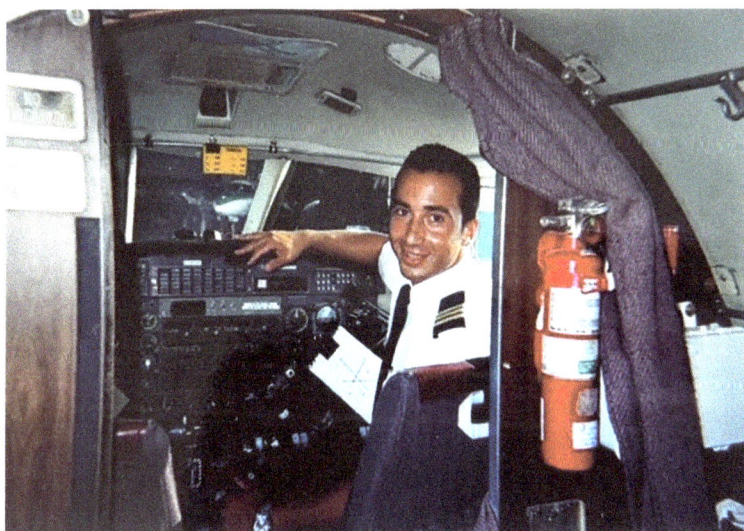

Perimeter Aviation ramp Winnipeg, Manitoba. 2000

FLYING IN NORTHERN CANADA

Line indoctrination training was a more relaxing stage of training. Although I was still required to do well and pass it, the learning environment was more easy-going and fun than the initial type-rating training, where constant malfunctions and failures occurred.

Perimeter Aviation serves the northern communities by providing regularly scheduled flights and cargo operations. Their passengers traveled from the northern communities to Winnipeg and back, but Perimeter would also fly doctors, nurses, dentists, engineers, hydro employees, police and RCMP officers, other professionals, and tourists as well that were heading up north to the fishing camps. I was fortunate to fly to the northern Indigenous reserves, meet and make friendships with great people, and have the opportunity to see beautiful places in Northern Canada that many people never get the chance to see. Northern Manitoba and Ontario have hundreds of islands and lakes. The views from the air and ground were beautiful to witness.

In northern Manitoba and Ontario, most airports we would fly to had a single gravel runway between 2900–4000 feet by 75 feet. Yes, we would land a Metroliner, an aircraft that has a reference landing speed (VREF) of 113 knots and an approach speed of 140 knots, on a gravel strip less than 4000 feet long—not to mention in all weather conditions, whether hot summer days or cold winter conditions. Most runways were on islands with water on either side of the threshold; there was no room for errors.

Since the runways were short and made of gravel strips, the airplane had to be landed in a specific way so that the propeller blades would not get damaged from flying rocks. "Floating" the airplane over the runway would lead to a go-around. With no room for errors, there was no such thing as having a bad day at the office. Performing a short field landing right at the beginning of the runway was required; otherwise you'd risk not giving the airplane enough runway to stop, or worse, end up in the lake.

Every season would have its challenges. In the winter, the runways would get icy and slippery; in the spring, they'd get soft due to the ice and snow melting, creating lots of mud.

The challenges for pilots included flying an airplane that had a fast approach speed, weather conditions leading to gusty winds, and low visibility in the winter and summer smog. While averaging six to eight takeoffs and landings per day, pilots were required to stay very sharp and fight fatigue, as every phase of flight required supreme concentration.

While flying up north, I learned that a good approach equals a good landing. By flying by this golden rule, I could position the airplane to touch down at the beginning of the runway in the appropriate approach speed, enabling it to decelerate to taxi speed before the end of the runway. Consistency was key on every approach and landing.

If the airplane was flown too slow, it would get sluggish—not a situation a pilot wants to be in. The Metro airplane didn't have a large wingspan; therefore, it had to be flown fast. Only captains would land and take off on northern gravel runways, which meant this was the best classroom for first officers to learn by watching. As an FO, you are there to assist the captain in his/her duties and work as a team to safely operate the airplane, maintaining a productive and efficient operation. The first officer would land and take off on all paved runways. Tasks would always be shared, but if a situation arose, the captain would make the final decision.

My goal was to improve and learn on every flight, from the decisions made by the captains I flew with and from the various circumstances we were faced with as a crew on every flight. In my first year as an FO at Perimeter, I had flown 1083 hours!

On a typical day at Perimeter, I would get to work early, at around 5:00 to 6:00 a.m. and walk into the crew room to say hi to the captain I was flying with that day. Then I'd head to Dispatch to find out which aircraft registration we'd be flying before heading out onto the ramp for the walk-around.

If it was winter (-35°C, typical "Winterpeg" temperatures), the goal would be to rush out onto the ramp and grab the first Herman Nelson heating unit before anyone else would get their hands on it. There were always a few units available, but due to such cold temperatures, not many would have a successful start. Therefore, you'd grab one as soon as you could, wheel it to your airplane's front door (a good leg workout on snow/ice-covered ramps), take the two rubber tubes, and place one in the cabin and the other in the cockpit. If the airplane was parked outside overnight, the cockpit would be frozen stiff; therefore, the Herman was in high demand.

Approximately twenty to thirty minutes before departure, the ramp personnel would bring carts filled with passenger's bags and cargo to the airplane. Now if you wanted to depart on time, a good FO would help with loading the bags and cargo. About ten minutes before departure, the FO would head back to the crew room and let the captain know the airplane was ready.

The captain would then head to Dispatch, pick up the flight manifest and paperwork, and proceed to the airplane. The FO would remain by the stairs while the captain confirmed the passenger count and headed up to the cockpit to strap in and perform the before-start checklists. My job would then be to assist passengers up the stairs and help them settle in. Once everyone was on board, I would ensure the cargo door was well locked before closing the main cabin door.

The flight up north would usually last about an hour and ten minutes on average to a hub such as Island Lake Airport (YIV) or Norway House (YNE). A typical turnaround at a Northern airport was fifteen minutes. Once all passengers were out and safely in the terminal, we had fifteen minutes to turn the airplane around, unload and load all bags and cargo, clean the seat pockets, fuel, and de-ice the wings before we were off to the next airport, which was ten to fifteen minutes away.

This was done for an average of six to eight stops per day; sometimes ten stops would not be unusual. Most stops up north were fifteen minutes long, with one-hour stops in Winnipeg. With so many takeoffs and landings, most days were mentally and physically demanding.

First officers and captains at that time were getting paid per mile, which was 5.5 cents for an FO when I started. In my first year, I made $17,700. Nonetheless, I was flying and doing something I love. I worked with great people, and my flying experience was rewarding.

The final approach Runway 04, St. Theresa Point Airport (YST), Manitoba.

Unloading cargo and bags

At Perimeter, pilots would do all the flight planning required prior to the flight, evaluate the weather, and order fuel to be loaded. Up north, since the airspace and airports did not have Air Traffic Control or control towers, pilots would use air-to-air radio communications to maintain separation from other aircraft. Uncontrolled airspace procedures were a daily operation. Therefore, pilots had many tasks to perform on their own and had many additional responsibilities compared to airline flying, where pilots get a lot more support and help from advanced aircraft avionics. This made northern flying demanding, requiring great attention to detail.

The learning experience for a pilot flying up north is second to none. It forces pilots to learn how to deal with and operate in various difficult weather conditions. The flying skills and knowledge accumulated flying up north prepare pilots for any future airline flying.

In some countries in the world, pilots progress straight from flight school to an airline job flying large jets, such as the Airbus A321/A330 and Boeing 737/777, flying from and into big air-traffic-controlled airports and landing on long, paved runways via precision instrument approaches. The training is a high-level quality, but the learning path is different where it is more academic focused—unlike northern remote flying on smaller, less sophisticated airplanes, which requires more hands-on flying and practical learning.

Of course, any student pilot will be happy to start working on an airbus aircraft fresh out of school, which does happen today. Which is ok but, in my opinion, having the practical learning experience you get from flying in remote places and less sophisticated airplanes is very beneficial to build a solid base for a pilot's early career stage.

Flying is academic, but to become a well-rounded and confident pilot, you have to be able to make decisions and face challenging situations. This only comes from practice and hands-on learning. You wouldn't go from a go-kart straight to a Formula 1 Ferrari car before driving in a Formula 1 race; you need to work your way up by driving smaller, less advanced but more demanding cars so that you can face challenging situations that will prepare you for the extremely demanding, highly intense Formula 1 racing.

My goal was to become a captain; therefore, I used every flight as a learning experience and took mental notes from the decisions the captain I flew with made. For example, since captains did all the landings up north, we would join the circuit and runway depending on the weather and other factors. If there was a straight ninety-degree and twenty-five knots crosswind, then the captain would usually prefer to land with the wind from the right instead of from the left. The reason was that on the Metro, the center windshield was not heated and therefore would often become frosted. With a right crosswind, the captain would have full use of his front windshield, which was heated, instead of landing with the left crosswind and being stuck with a center windshield with not much visibility. Also, the control yoke was more comfortable in dealing with a right crosswind. This was one of the many techniques I memorized and put in my tool bag.

Some captains would even review with FOs aircraft systems and IFR procedures in cruise flight, which was a great way to share knowledge and something that I'd do later in my career as a captain.

Landing the Metro up north on short gravel strips was quite the challenge on any given day with nice weather conditions, but add darkness up north with no city lights or visual cues, and that was a different ball game.

The first time I landed up north was a memorable experience. We were lining up about twenty miles on final on to Runway 04 at St. Theresa Point Airport (YST). Although the captain I was flying with had said, "Runway in sight," I couldn't see anything out there, even though we were in the clear with no clouds anywhere ahead of us. All I saw was total darkness out the front windshield. As we got closer, I was able to make out some tiny lights ahead on the approach path.

"You mean, that's the runway there, twelve o'clock ahead?"

"Yup, that's the one!" he said.

I was amazed. Was this really the runway? We were flying at 140 knots speed on the final approach as we selected the flaps to slow us down to a landing reference speed of 113 knots. The runway looked as if it was lit up with 100-watt light bulbs. That first night landing was on a gravel strip 3391 feet by 75 feet long.

As we got closer to the airport, I was able to see it and the runway environment. The captain held the nose up from the runway after touching down the main wheels. While doing that, with the right hand, the captain would turn the landing lights switch off. The final step was to gently put the nose gear down on the gravel runway so as not to spray rocks and damage the belly of the airplane. That was our technique.

The Metro had its landing lights right in the middle of the fuselage's belly, protruding forward in line behind the nose gear. If the night-landing technique was not executed quickly and in the correct order, after touchdown the nose gear wheels would spray rocks and gravel right onto the protruding landing lights, damaging them.

Since night landings up north lacked the visual cues pilots usually have when landing in big city airports, we had to always use the "3:1 rule of descent" technique to ensure the approach was made on a correct flight profile. In the "3:1 rule of descent," three miles of travel should be allowed for every 1,000 feet (300 m) descent. I have used that formula on the descent and approaches flying up north and on all the airplanes I flew later in my career.

The final approach Runway 22, St. Theresa Point Airport (YST), Manitoba.

Prior to takeoff, runway 04, St. Theresa Point Airport (YST), Manitoba.

The final approach to runway 05, Oxford House Airport (YOH), Manitoba

EDUCATION AND DREAMS
HAVE NO PRICE TAGS

I received a phone call on my cell one day just before heading out on a flight. It was the bank I received my student loan from. It had been two years since I graduated, and it was time to pay my student loan. The call was to set up a pre-authorized payment plan. The amount I had to pay was a minimum of $860 per month.

My salary on average was just under $1000 a month. After paying rent, car insurance, and groceries, I didn't have much money leftover and knew that sometimes I had even run out of money before the next paycheck. But the agent on the phone demanded a minimum of $860 per month.

The schedule at Perimeter was busy, and even if I wanted to work somewhere else to make an extra income, I wouldn't be able to keep both jobs. I tried to negotiate with the bank and asked them for some more time, but I was told if I didn't make the payments, the account would have to be transferred to a collection agency.

I didn't know much about collection agencies, but I soon found out. It was the most horrible, stressful, degrading, and aggressive treatment I had ever received. I always had the intention to pay the loan back, but at that time, I wasn't able to make such high payments.

After my conversation with the agent, I headed to the airplane, putting the conversation behind me. I had no choice; I had another four flights ahead of me and knew that the quicker I put aside that conversation, the better I would feel.

The loan eventually got transferred to a collection agency, and as nice as I can put it, dealing with a collection agency was a very bad experience. They loved calling me. I'm sure that they were trained or pressured to get payments from whomever they were calling, but the fact was they called often, refusing to understand that I didn't have the money at that time, nor would I the next day or the next month. The fact that I had nothing I could sell or anyone I could borrow money from didn't mean anything to them; they kept harassing me on a weekly, sometimes daily, basis.

Eventually, almost half a year and many conversations later, I was able to negotiate and convince the agency to accept $50 monthly payments, and then not long after, $150 monthly payments. This was just enough to pay a portion of the interest, which was on average 3–5% on a $65,000 student loan, but at least I was able to stop the agency from continually calling and bugging me.

My payments eventually went up to $400 per month. I had fought very hard for a few years to have my student loan transferred back to the Ministry of Education. I didn't want to keep dealing with the collection agency.

As my career progressed and I had better salaries, I was able to pay the remaining sum of my student loan in full directly to the Ministry of Education. I haven't done the calculations, but I believe with all the interests accumulated and the years that I wasn't able to make any payments, I probably paid close to $100,000 in student loan debt. But then again, that was the price I had to pay. If not for the student loan, I would not have been able to work in this amazing profession and make a living in this industry.

Today, in 2021, the total cost of pilot training has gone up significantly, but regardless, this amount should not prevent anyone from pursuing a flying career, or any other profession. I believe studying something you are passionate about has no price tag, and when someone is unable to get financial help from family or unable to save enough, then a student loan is there for that reason. I see a student loan as an investment for their future. The important thing to remember is to do thorough research about the conditions of the loan, the reimbursement plan, the time frame to repay, and the interest rates.

I learned from a young age that money brings you things you desire. When I was nine or ten years old, when the school year ended, I decided to sell the schoolbooks I didn't need anymore. With whatever little money I made, I bought myself lunch and kept the rest. It wasn't much money at all, but the lesson I learned was that money brings opportunities and gains.

In 2017, when I paid the final balance of the student loan, I felt a great sense of accomplishment and was glad that I had made the right decision twenty years ago to take on that big student loan.

Without student loans, it would have been difficult to study such a costly profession, or any other profession for that matter, unless I had the chance to save or financial help. My advice is, if you can get the loan, take it—borrow as much as you can!

Airbus A330, Lisbon, Portugal, July 2019.

HELLO, THIS IS YOUR CAPTAIN SPEAKING

During my first year at Perimeter Airlines, I flew 1083 hours, which is just under the 1200 maximum allowable hours by regulations. That was a busy year, with lots of flying, which I enjoyed very much. The milestone I'm very proud of achieving was the 1000-hour mark, which I achieved on November 27, 2000. That total hour's mark was always the magic number to have, as most companies always asked for that minimum. The next milestone I was aiming for was 5000, and then the big 10,000 hours.

During that first year flying on the Metro, I learned a lot about hand-flying skills, aviation regulations, in-flight weather knowledge, flight planning, instrument flying rules, working in a crew environment, and of course, the Metro II airplane. I had the chance to fly through the four seasons in Manitoba and learned how to operate the airplane in each of these seasons.

At Perimeter, as with most airlines, every year a pilot undergoes a flight test where they are evaluated on different malfunctions and must perform upper air work, various approaches, and drills. Besides being the regulation's requirement, it is also an opportunity for the chief pilot to maintain standards, evaluate the training program, and amend procedures as needed.

Knowing that my first recurrent flight test was coming up in a couple of months, I started my preparation in advance. I reviewed all my drills, aircraft systems, and went over different flight test scenarios. I wanted to make sure I did very well.

A few weeks before my recurrent flight training and test, the chief pilot informed me that I was going to do my training as a captain. I was so happy and pumped about this amazing news. I began to study on every day off and spent countless hours "hangar flying," going over all my drills and getting my hands accustomed to all the switches and knobs on the captain's side of the flight deck.

There I was on March 14, 2001, just a year after getting hired, with Mark back in the cockpit again and I in the captain seat. My upgrade training was a special moment for me, as I was able to go flying with Mark, the person who gave me that first opportunity.

The training flight with Mark went very well, and the next day I completed the captain PPC Pilot Proficiency Check (PPC) Flight Test with the operations manager. With the flight test completed, I hit another self-milestone I was proud to have accomplished.

I started captain line indoctrination training on April 2, 2001, on the Winnipeg to St. Theresa Point flight. Captain line indoctrination is performed on a normal revenue flight, with passengers on board, and the trainee flies with a highly experienced training captain. On that flight, the training captain teaches, reviews, and evaluates the candidate on every stage of the flight. On those flights, the objective is to learn and demonstrate knowledge, leadership, decision-making, and aircraft knowledge, while—most importantly—working safely and being operational. On those flights I took as much information and knowledge from the training pilot as I could, taking notes which I would review during the evenings after my flights.

I had the opportunity to fly many times during my captain line training flights with Ron, one of the company's training captains. Ron had lots of northern flying experience and on the Metro as well. I liked Ron's way of teaching and the examples he would use, as he'd always back them up with data, research, or real events. He taught me, for example, how to analyze the color of the gravel on the runway to be able to determine if the runway is too soft, which often occurs during the springtime.

He taught me techniques but also survival skills, such as knowing what to watch for during flying and the operations of flying up north so as not to get caught in a bad situation or an undesirable state. For example, we reviewed approach speed calculations during icing conditions. He showed me how and why to spray the landing gear wheel rollers to prevent them from freezing during the winter months.

Once these rollers would freeze, it could prevent the landing gear from extending normally, which eventually leads to an emergency gear extension.

Flying up north with the Metro aircraft was a rewarding but very demanding experience, with no room for errors. The training I received was excellent and gave me all the tools I needed to be able to operate safely and efficiently up north.

After I completed my captain line training, I was released for my first flight as Metro II captain on May 4, 2001, with a total time of 1453 hours. The flight was a cargo run from Winnipeg International Airport to Fargo, North Dakota airport (KFAR), and then on to Thief River Falls Regional Airport (KTVF).

The airline had the policy to let new captains fly the cargo routes for a few months until an opening to fly up north came up. This built captain time, as we'd be able to get used to the left seat and flying in and out of airports with long paved asphalt runways before facing the gravel strips up north. Also, since most of the cargo flights were at night, it was a good opportunity to get a feel for night flying.

I was on the cargo run for a few months, and on July 19, 2001, I flew my first flight to the northern community Norway House (YNE), landing for the first time on a gravel strip officially as the captain.

A RUNWAY DOES NOT GET SHORTER THAN THIS

Most of the Manitoba airports up north had considerably short gravel runways, averaging 3500 feet. But there was one airport the airline had regular service to on the Metro II that had a very short runway: Berens River Airport (YBV).

Berens River Airport (YBV) is about a forty-five-minute flight from Winnipeg. Its gravel/crushed-rock runway is in a 09/27 direction and is just under 2900 feet (884 meters) long. The approach to runway 27 is straightforward, with no obstacles or terrain. But by the threshold of Runway 09, there's a small building (a hotel) right on the approach path. Now if the winds favored Runway 09, you had no choice but to use it to take advantage of all available performances landing into wind.

Once the aircraft overflew the hotel, the technique we used was to drop and touch down right at the beginning of the runway, without wasting any runway length. The approach to Runway 09 was challenging on a perfect weather day, let alone when some gusty winds and weather were added to the mix. New captains were restricted to that airport and needed specific training before getting released. Mastering the approach and landing at YBV was very rewarding, to say the least!

MAYDAY

Operating up north was more than just flying; pilots were also managing a business and had a big part of the airline's daily operations. Within the major airlines, many tasks are handled by various departments, but in the north, pilots had many more tasks.

When I started flying up north, most approaches to the airport during low visibility and IFR conditions were performed using non-precision approaches (NPA). These were approaches that had no vertical guidance signal, where pilots needed to manage the descent and altitude manually, and the final approach course was followed by a radial or tracks. With the introduction of GPS navigation systems in the aircraft a few years later, the approaches were a lot easier to perform and much more precise, enabling straight-in approaches to a runway.

November 15, 2001 was the first time in my career that I had to deal with an emergency. Flying aircraft C-FIHB, we were established on the final approach to Runway 27 at God's River Airport (ZGI). As we were breaking out from the overcast layer, I was able to start seeing the runway up ahead.

"Gear down," I called, as we were approaching the final descent to the runway.

As the FO placed the landing gear handle to the down position, the nose gear position indicator did not illuminate a green light showing that it was down and locked; it only showed that the gear was in transit. The FO tried another cycle but with no success—the nose gear indication would not show a safe position.

"Go-around!" I called.

We climbed to a safe altitude before troubleshooting the technical problem. Once leveled, we brought the gear up and down but still had no positive confirmation that the gear was down and locked. There was a way to verify if the nose gear was out from the wheel well. Since the engine spinner was buffed and shiny, it would mirror the gear, so we used that to see if the nose gear was out from the wheel well, which it was, but we needed to be certain that it was locked. Without that confirmation, the nose gear could collapse after touchdown.

It was the first time I had to deal with such an abnormal situation. Everything in my short aviation career up to this point went smoothly, without any major aircraft technical failures. I had to remain calm and make sure one of us was flying the aircraft while the other dealt with checklists and communications.

"Bingo Fuel" is military slang for the minimum fuel required to return to base or, in our case, an alternate airport, keeping in mind reserve fuel on top of the minimum to the alternate fuel. After reviewing the emergency gear checklist and considering the remaining fuel on board, we decided to head to Thompson Airport (YTH), which wasn't our filed alternate airport. Our alternate airport was closer to our position, but the decision to divert to a further airport was for a few reasons. First, Thompson had a paved runway instead of gravel, which would be a safer place to land in case the nose gear collapsed. Also, Thompson Airport had emergency vehicles, which we needed to assist us in case the nose gear did not support the airplane.

The passengers were briefed about the technical state of the aircraft and informed that we had to head to YTH. Also, in a situation like this, we ensured that no passengers were sitting in the front row seats by the propeller. If the nose gear ever collapsed, that could result in the props striking the ground and sending metal parts through the fuselage and into the cabin. Therefore, to prevent anyone from getting hurt, we made sure no one sat in those seats.

We did a flyover the airport's control tower so that the flight service personnel would be able to see the position of the nose gear, which they confirmed was out and extended. Also, the emergency vehicles were in position as well; not taking any risks, we had declared an emergency. As per the manufacturer's recommended procedures, we performed the emergency gear extension, and the landing was made by gently putting the nose gear onto the runway, which to our luck remained locked. The outcome of the flight was resolved safely.

The lessons we learned from this emergency situation: flying the airplane is always top priority; know your position and where you are heading at all times; perform a go-around maneuver when things are not right or unsafe; climb to a safe altitude before doing any troubleshooting; work as a team; and most importantly, stay calm. Always be aware of the fuel status. These valuable lessons helped me in other inflight situations later in my career.

A BUSY CIRCLING APPROACH

It was the middle of winter, late afternoon, and we were on our last flight of the day, heading up north to St. Theresa Point Airport. We planned a short stop—offload/board passengers, load bags, fuel, and de-ice—before flying back to Winnipeg, which would have completed our eleven-hour duty day.

The weather forecast was just above weather minimums, with snow showers in the forecast as well. We were planning the GPS area navigation (RNAV) stand-alone approach. RNAV approach is a non-precision approach based solely on the use of the GPS navigation receivers; it is a more accurate navigation approach, not relying on any ground-based antennas. Also, this straight-in approach reduces the workload on the pilots: hardly any turns are required and it provides the opportunity to be lined up with the runway at least ten miles back.

We were on the descent and navigating to the initial approach fix (IAF), where the instrument approach would commence. Suddenly the "Check RAIM" message came on the GPS display, which was not good news. RAIM stands for Receiver Autonomous Integrity Monitoring, which provides integrity monitoring before and during the GPS approach. It monitors everything in the onboard equipment that is required during the approach, ensuring it is functioning accordingly. For a GPS receiver to perform RAIM or fault detection (FD) function, a minimum number of satellites need to be utilized for satisfactory geometry.

Since the GPS was not working correctly, we needed to cancel the approach and climb to a safe altitude of 3000 feet. Once leveled, we reviewed and I briefed the non-directional radio beacon (NDB) approach, which is a more demanding approach and not as accurate as the GPS RNAV approach, leading us to perform a circling approach. A circling maneuver is required whenever no straight-in minima are published or when the approach flown does not serve the runway of the intended landing.

The weather that evening met the company's minimum requirement for this kind of approach. It was windy with crosswinds and blowing snow. At that time, St. Theresa Point Airport did not have the best runway lighting system, which at times seemed as if 100-watt light bulbs were used to light up the runway. The runway lighting has improved a lot since.

Safety first! During the circling approach, the aerodrome had to always remain in sight while I monitored the airplane's altitude, speed, and bank angle throughout the maneuver. Crew coordination is vital to safe and effective circling, and that is where the great assistance of my FO came in. While I focused on looking outside and keeping the runway in sight through the snow showers, my FO focused on the flight instruments, making sure I was maintaining a safe speed, altitude, and not overbanking the aircraft.

It was a challenging flight maneuver, requiring full concentration. There was no room for any error. I had to keep the runaway in sight; therefore I had to set the correct torque power setting on the engines and have the flight controls fully trimmed. This was what pure flying is all about. I felt connected to a machine, as if it was an extension of my body.

I couldn't keep the aircraft wide enough from the runway on the first circling maneuver due to the blowing winds pushing us through the final approach path to Runway 04. I had to be perfectly lined up with the runway before descending from the circling altitude. Jack, my FO, and I both had the fuel endurance on our minds, knowing that once the fuel quantity would reach 750 pounds, we would have to head to our alternate airport. We had enough for one more circling maneuver, and I was glad we took extra fuel for any additional approaches since we knew the weather wasn't good up north that evening.

Back again, overhead the airport for the second circling maneuver, I turned to the northwest and one more left-hand pattern. On this second try, I was able to widen out my base leg and turn a couple of seconds earlier than I did on the first approach, which allowed the left crosswind to help me line up perfectly on Runway 04. I called for final flaps and touched down at a reference speed (VREF) of 115 knots, which included a couple of extra knots for gusts. After landing, I thanked my FO for his assistance during the approach.

Flying as a crew compared to single pilot has great benefits. This approach gave me confidence in my hand-flying abilities but also in my knowledge of our operations. I was now ready to face bigger challenges to share my knowledge with other pilots, and to become an instructor and check pilot.

INSTRUCTOR PILOT

In March 2003, I was promoted to an instructor (training pilot) position on the Metro II. I had never pursued an instructor rating in flight college but always had a passion for teaching and sharing my knowledge. I am fortunate to have watched and learned from the great instructors I've worked with in my career to date. It was rewarding to give new company pilots the tools to succeed in training, just as some pilots had done with me. Also, the opportunity to grow as a pilot and to be part of the training department of the airline was something I was looking forward to.

As the assistant to the training manager, I would give initial training to newly hired pilots and prepare them for their Pilot Proficiency Check Flight Test (PPC); just as Mark did with me when I was hired. I was also assigned to give recurrent and captain upgrade training.

Since training required record keeping, I was also responsible for the pilot's training files to ensure all training was assigned and documented. This taught me a lot about how an airline training department worked, how to be organized, and the importance of being detailed with paperwork.

The schedule fluctuated and required working on weekends, early morning hours, and late nights, when night training had to be given. This position also involved many hours of administrative work in the training department office. It was overall a great experience and an opportunity to advance but also to evolve as a pilot besides just flying from point A to B.

As a training pilot, I became more proficient with air regulations. Also, teaching and being constantly "in the books" allowed me to become a more technical pilot. When you teach, you also learn at the same time.

But being a training pilot can come with great risk as well. During my experience, all the training was done in the airplane since the flight simulator wasn't available yet at that time; therefore, training involved flying with pilots who had low experience, just like I once had. Also, training new captains in a seat they are not accustomed to requires the instructor to do a lot of work. Not only do the aircraft's limitations have to be observed and always respected but also the training airspace has to be well maintained. A training pilot has to watch out for traffic and communicate with Air Traffic Control, all while teaching and ensuring their candidates are learning in a comfortable learning environment.

As an instructor teaching live on the airplane, you have to know your limits and how much you are willing to allow a candidate to perform before correcting them so that they can observe the aircraft's limitations without exceeding company procedures or risking a flight violation. It's easy to do that in the simulator as there are no risks involved, but in the airplane it's a different ball game.

An instructor pilot needs to be very comfortable with the airplane, patient, calm, and able to pass on the information to pilots with very different backgrounds and experiences. Every person learns and grasps information in a different way, and it's up to an instructor to adapt to everyone's learning capabilities. You can teach pilots lots of theory, but it's in practicing and doing exercises hands-on that they learn the most. Simulators are perfect tools for that.

I had the opportunity to work with Ron, who was the training manager at the airline. He and I had a chance to fly together when I was doing my captain upgrade training, where I learned a lot from him. Our teaching style was similar and, in some ways, very different, which allowed us to share ideas and decide on training scenarios and techniques together. I appreciated the trust and confidence he had in me. The aviation industry is unique, in a way, as knowledge and techniques are passed on from one pilot generation to the next.

Through my position as a training pilot, I learned that even though my student pilots were flying the same airplane and following the same procedures, I had to use a variety of ways to explain or teach something to them. Sometimes, the first approach or explanation is not well understood; in that case, an instructor must have the ability to find another approach with different examples to help the candidate understand an exercise or a specific topic. Because of that, an instructor must be patient and able to think outside the box.

Safety when it comes to training in the airplane is always the number one priority. Second, the instructor must be focused at all times and have excellent situational awareness—there is not much room for error.

★   ★   ★

I was conducting a night-training flight once for a newly hired pilot, where they had to perform five takeoffs and landings through touch-and-go approaches. Performing a good touchdown and landing is achieved by executing a controlled and stabilized approach. The flare—which is that gradual pitch-up maneuver just before touchdown—slows the descent and allows the airplane to settle nicely on the runway. Flare too high or too fast and the aircraft drops abruptly, which could lead to a hard landing or an excess runway length. Flare too low or not enough, and you'll land hard or flat.

The first night landing wasn't the smoothest or gentlest, but as the landings progressed, the pilot was improving by making small corrections and fine-tuning what they had learned from the last approach and landing. We were on the fifth and last approach, and I was expecting it to go very well since the progression was positive—but things went completely different. Just as we were crossing the threshold, the pilot was flaring slightly high and their reaction, unexpectedly, was to push forward and hard on the control column. It could have been night illusions or not being well-trimmed, but regardless, I had a half-second to react or we would have hit the nose gear hard on the ground or, even worse, have it collapse.

My hands were always on my lap, close to the control wheel, on all training flights during landings, so I was able to put some back pressure on the controls and assist the pilot in training to land on the main landing gear. Had I not been ready, the outcome would have been different. When teaching on an airplane, the risk is always present and being focused and alert is a must. A hard landing in the sim might hurt the ego, but in an airplane it can cause a lot of damage.

★   ★   ★

Since many airports up north still had backup non-directional beacon (NDB) approaches in case airplanes weren't equipped with a GPS, we always included NDB approaches in training to keep pilots proficient—and no better place to practice than at St. Andrews Airport (YAV), just a few miles north of Winnipeg. Since the NDB approaches didn't line up the aircraft with any of the three runways at YAV, the circling approach was necessary after completing the NDB approach.

I was giving a training flight early Sunday morning, with a few Cessna airplanes already in the circuit pattern practicing touch-and-go landings, and we were approaching the airport from the east at 140 knots, almost three times the speed of the Cessnas, about to commence our circling approach maneuver to line up with Runway 36. This was a challenging exercise for a new captain and for me, the instructor, as well, as I was sitting on the right seat and we were circling to the left on the captain trainee side.

I looked in and out of the cockpit, ensuring circling altitude and minimum speed were maintained through the maneuver. To simulate a single-engine approach, this exercise was performed with the left engine at idle thrust. The exercise was to complete the circling maneuver, line up to Runway 36 in the landing configuration, and perform a go-around, where both engines would be used.

As we turned final to Runway 36, the candidate realized that the airplane was slightly high on the approach. Instead of performing the go-around maneuver, the candidate cut the power on the right engine—something we called "chopping the power." When "chopping" engine power on a turboprop airplane, the airplane will drop and lose altitude very quickly. When power is cut in such a way, the feeling and sound is sinking and alarming at the same time.

I immediately took control and pitched the airplane nose up while pushing forward the power levers to full takeoff power. The good thing about the turboprop airplane versus a jet is that go-around power from the engines is available with not much lag, whereas on a jet airplane it could take a few long seconds before power is being produced.

We climbed to a safe altitude and returned to the home base airport for another approach and a full stop. We had a debrief on the session, and as alarming as the experience was, it was a very important and valuable lesson for the candidate. Training is all about learning. Also, another reminder for me that anything can happen anytime during a training flight.

Flying is all about energy management and always being aware of the airplane's inertia. The airplane's energy condition or state is a function of the following airplane's flight parameters: airspeed, altitude, drag, and thrust. The pilot's job is to control and handle the aircraft's energy by balancing the airspeed, drag/thrust, and the flight path to maintain a stabilized approach.

Cutting power abruptly on any aircraft—whether a piston, turboprop, or jet—should never be done. If a pilot decides to cut power during an approach, a wiser decision instead would be to go around, come back, and perform a second, better-managed approach.

Most flights go on smooth and uneventful, but sometimes things happen unexpectedly and sometimes without much warning. I had a few more interesting flights in my career.

CAN'T SEE AHEAD

It was the middle of winter and blowing snow conditions. The weather was right at landing minimums of 200 feet overcast and half-mile visibility during the approach. With this weather in mind, we would see the runway in the last few seconds of the approach after breaking out from the overcast cloud layer. We were on the instrument approach system (ILS) approach to Runway 36 at Winnipeg. I was at the controls flying the approach while my FO, Jason, was talking with the tower to get the weather update report. Jason was one of the cargo loaders I met on the ramp a few years back when I was loading the cargo airplane, and here we were flying together. Aviation is a small world!

On our final approach on the ILS, I focused on the flight instruments, making sure the airplane was lined up with the runway by making small corrections on the control wheel. On an ILS approach, a pilot follows a vertical and horizontal bar on the primary flight display instrument. By keeping both bars in a cross by using pitch and thrust corrections, the airplane could be perfectly lined up with the runway.

As we were approaching 200 feet above ground, I was getting ready to transition from scanning my flight instruments to looking through the windshield to find the runway lights. I looked for runway visual cues that would allow me to continue the approach visually to the touchdown zone.

"Minimums!" Jason called out at the decision altitude (DA).

"Runway in sight. Continue," I called, flying visually, looking outside for the last 200 feet.

The transition from the minimum decision height of 200 feet and half-mile visibility to the time the airplane touches down happens very quickly; therefore, it is best to keep the airplane as trimmed as it's been for the last few minutes and not make any big corrections. Otherwise any trim or major power changes will make the airplane deviate from the stable approach path.

Half-mile visibility is not much when traveling over the runway threshold at 115 knots (212 km/h), with blowing snow and a strong crosswind. As we touched down on the runway and decelerated the airplane, the blowing snow intensified, causing the visibility to get continually worse as we traveled down the runway. For the last three to five seconds of the deceleration, I couldn't see straight ahead of the windshield anymore due to the reduced visibility. I had to make sure we remained centered on the runway. I instinctively looked to my left and was able to see the white runway edge lights, which helped us remain on the runway and away from the runway edge. It's amazing how it only takes a few seconds for a calm and uneventful one-and-a-half-hour flight to turn into a pure adrenaline rush.

The tower had to help and guide us so that we could safely exit the active runway and get on a taxiway. Once on the taxiway, we waited a few minutes for the snowfall to move before continuing to slowly taxi to the parking ramp.

Winnipeg's winter weather, in general, has clear skies with many sunny days. But what makes it challenging is the strong wind, which can produce very low windchill conditions that can feel below -30°C or sometimes even below -50°C.

On another occasion, on a different flight and with a different FO, I was on the ILS approach to the longest runway in Winnipeg: Runway 36. The weather was right at weather minimums, and we were the second in sequence, with a third company flight behind us. As we got to 200 feet—the lowest altitude we could descend to before having visual contact—all we could see through the thick fog was distracting city and airport lights. I couldn't make out the runway lights and decided to pull up and go around. We flew the missed approach procedure and continued to the alternate airport at Brandon, Manitoba.

It was the first time I witnessed illusions created by lights flashing through a thick fog. These illusions could cause the pilot to become disoriented and, if not recognized early, can make the pilot maneuver the airplane into an unsafe position. That flight was a reminder to always trust the flight instruments and that situational awareness must be maintained at all times.

When performing a go-around maneuver from an approach, the focus is to attain and maintain a positive rate of climb, and trust and follow your instruments. Vestibular/somatogyral illusions are dangerous and can confuse pilots. A pilot should believe and trust what they see on their flight instruments and not what they "feel" the airplane is doing.

STUCK WITH A SNOWMOBILE

We were on a typical duty day with eight flights planned for the day. On our way to St. Theresa Point Airport that afternoon, we were looking forward to the one-hour break on the ground before another departure. To have such a long break up north was very rare, as usually we would stop for fifteen minutes, just enough to turn the airplane around and continue the next departure.

The Metro had a large aft cargo door where it was possible to load big and bulky items. That day, we had a big snowmobile that, by using a forklift, our cargo loaders were able to fit in the cargo compartment in Winnipeg.

After landing up north and disembarking the passengers, my FO Chris and I proceeded to the back of the airplane to offload the snowmobile. It was -30°C that day, with strong northern winds that afternoon. I was crunched inside the aircraft's cargo compartment while Chris was outside standing on a large baggage cart. I couldn't maneuver and twist the snowmobile enough to get it out the cargo door; the fact that you couldn't stand upright inside the cargo compartment of the Metro didn't help. With a forklift in Winnipeg, it was easier to move the snowmobile on a pallet, but without the forklift up north and being inside the airplane bent over with very little room made it impossible to move the snowmobile.

After a few attempts, we had no choice but to remove and detach parts from the back of the snowmobile to give us some room to maneuver it inside the cargo compartment; otherwise this thing would not come out. With the cargo door open, blowing cold winds, and bare hands, disassembling the snowmobile was just not fun.

It took us exactly an hour to eventually remove the snowmobile from the airplane and put the parts back on it. Once that was all done, we looked at each other, both frozen and laughing about the experience.

"We are freezing our butts here, Chris, but one day we will be sitting in a big jet enjoying a nice cup of coffee on our way to Europe and will be thinking about this day," I told Chris.

There were many moments later in my career that reminded me of this cold day and made me appreciate the sacrifices we pilots made to get ahead in our careers.

CHAPTER 5

✈

THE MAJOR AIRLINES ARE HIRING

I had always wanted to fly wide-body jet airplanes to international destinations. I was fascinated with their size, capability, engineering achievement, and the adventure of flying long-haul flights over oceans and continents. Also, travel has always been one of my biggest passions in life, and I couldn't wait for the day when I would have the opportunity to fly to different parts of the globe and discover new places I had never been to.

To have the opportunity to fly for a major airline in the early 2000s required a solid flight experience. The airline industry has two very different hiring periods: major hiring spree or no hiring at all, and even the possibility for layoffs. For those who want to go that route, when major airlines are going through a hiring spree, it is time to jump in the race and get a spot. Some prefer to stay with their regional or small carrier, which is a perfectly good decision as well. Each pilot needs to evaluate the pros and cons of working for a major airline, like in any other profession.

I sent my CV to Air Transat as soon as I became a captain with Perimeter in the beginning of 2001. I didn't have the minimum required hours yet, but I figured I would send an updated résumé every six months as I built more experience. Some may disagree with the practice of sending a résumé before meeting the minimum requirements of an airline, but I cannot say there's a better way to go around that, unless the airline specifically advertises not to send résumés prematurely. Although I have seen airlines hire below the required minimums, it all depends on the shape of the industry—if there is a shortage of pilots or an abundance.

Most pilots at the beginning of 2000 would spend two to four years at a small airline (what we call third level) and then move on to the regional carriers or major airlines overseas. The average total flight time for pilots who left the small carriers ranged from 2500 to 3500 hours. Some made a long-term career at the small carriers and were happy not dealing with the hustle of jetlag or overseas flying, whereas others decided to move on to regional carriers.

When the tragedy of September 11, 2001 happened, everything in aviation came to a halt. The airlines did not do any hiring for a while, and many even had layoffs. The industry was greatly affected with many airlines going bankrupt. Many pilots didn't really know when and if they would even fly again. We depend a lot on our career, which is one very sensitive to the global condition. It is the first industry affected when there is a world crisis and the last one to recover. It's an industry where profits are hard to make, and any global situation affected by safety or fuel prices, for example, will directly influence its profitability and sustainability.

Although I was very lucky and fortunate to be able to continue flying after the 9/11 attacks, as opposed to many other unfortunate pilots who lost their jobs, it was the first time in my short aviation career that I witnessed how volatile and unpredictable my career is. One day you could have a job, and the next day you could be unemployed.

Major airlines overseas and regional carriers in Canada restarted hiring in 2004–2005, and many pilots took the opportunity to apply. I decided to do the same. I was ready for a new challenge in my career and the chance to fly a more advanced airplane, perhaps a jet. I was also open to living in another city or a different country overseas. I believe a pilot should progress in their career, whether it is to fly a bigger, more challenging aircraft, seek promotions in the airline, or gain experience flying on other routes or destinations.

I applied to the two major airlines in Canada, one regional carrier, and one major airline overseas, which was hiring many pilots at that time. The application process for the airline overseas was two-stage at that time. First, you were invited for an interview, which in my case took place in San Francisco. Once successful, you were then invited overseas for the second stage, which was a lot more demanding and a lengthier process. At that time, the airline operated only wide-body aircraft, such as the Boeing 747/777 and Airbus A330/A340; therefore, the interview process focused on the candidate's personality, ability to work in a team environment, and skills, with a strong emphasis on technical knowledge, aircraft systems, meteorology, and aerodynamics. The application process was thorough and extensive. I was invited for the pilot interview not long after submitting my application and had almost three months to prepare. I was very happy to be invited and for the opportunity to work for such a prestigious airline.

I made myself a study plan where I wrote down all the various topics I needed to review to prepare myself. I made a list of the documents, publications, and books I planned to read and review before the first-stage interview. I made myself a list of everything I needed to do, such as the documents I needed to prepare, the suit and briefcase I needed to purchase, and so on, and included the deadlines I had to meet so that everything would be done before the interview.

I researched and read anything I could find about the interview process and the airline so that I would be well prepared to succeed in their process. There were some forums on the web that I took notes from. Pilots would ask questions and other pilots would reply, and I found the information very helpful. You still had to be careful not to believe everything you read, but more information was better than none. Thanks to the Internet!

It was highly recommended to read the book *Handling the Big Jets* by David P. Davies (1973), which was fundamental to be well familiar with since many interview questions at that time referred to the information in that book. I read the book twice.

I also booked a practice interview with a Canadian company that offered interview practice sessions. It wasn't necessary, but since I hadn't done many airline interviews, I found it helpful, especially because it was an interview prep company familiar with the airline's interview process.

To help me practice for an interview with a group panel, I tore up pictures of random faces from a magazine and stuck them on the wall in front of my desk at home. When I practiced answering my interview questions, I would look at those faces and practice making good eye contact.

The evening shift after work, studying for the interview.

The interview process was demanding and challenging, so I wanted to make sure I was overprepared. I had to manage my time between work and studying. After a typical flying day with a ten- to twelve-hour duty time, I would come home, have dinner, and study for the interview till late at night. On weekends, I would give training flights. This was my routine for three months; any social life was nonexistent.

I arrived in San Francisco a day before my interview and stayed in a hotel within walking distance from the office where my interview would be held.

The next day, I arrived to the interview fifteen minutes early. I introduced myself with a big smile to the friendly receptionist despite feeling nervous for what was coming ahead.

The interview panel consisted of a captain/ops manager and an HR representative. I had a chance to talk about myself and my career in a very comfortable interview environment. The interview questions were very technical; my answers had to include examples and explanations. For example, I was given a flight situation and had to answer by explaining my train of thought and how I arrived at my answer.

It was my first interview with a major airline, and although I was well prepared, I didn't have much interview experience. I couldn't self-analyze how I was doing during the interview, which may have been a good thing. Although I was well prepared, I was definitely nervous.

After leaving the airline's office, I felt relieved the interview was done. It was a long three months of studying and not knowing what to expect, and now it was finally over!

Not long after the interview in San Francisco, I was invited overseas for the second stage of the interview process, and again I had almost three months to prepare. I was super happy and excited—after all my preparation, effort, and time, to receive such great news was a rewarding feeling. I was informed that at the second stage, there would also be a simulator evaluation on the Boeing 747-400, a group exercise with an evaluation team, a thorough medical exam, and an interview as well.

Although the Metro is a demanding aircraft, where good handling skills can be learned and developed, it is a very different machine than the mighty 747. First, the 747 is a big jet and has all-glass cockpit instrumentation and four engines. I knew that the simulator evaluation would be a very important part of the process; I had to be well prepared for that.

The airline sent all the candidates the flight profile that we would be expected to fly and evaluate using a Full Flight Simulator. On September 23, 2005, a couple of months before the interview, I flew to Vancouver, BC, where a 747-100 simulator was available for pilots to rent. I had the opportunity to fly the simulator for about an hour and practice the flight profile. Although the -100 was different and not as advanced as the -400-simulator model used in the evaluation, it was still very good practice.

A month before leaving overseas, I drove from Winnipeg to Minneapolis to a major simulator training center. I booked a one-hour simulator session with an instructor on the Boeing 747-400. The session cost $1000 US, but despite being very pricey, I knew it was an investment I had to make.

To keep myself awake and entertained on the long road trip to Minneapolis, I brought with me a small cassette tape that I previously recorded of myself answering key interview questions. I had read that hearing yourself answering questions was a good way to remember the delivery of the answers.

I met up with the sim instructor one late evening in November 2005. We went over the flight profile, and he briefed me on the cockpit switches, instrumentation, and the flight characteristics of the airplane. The B747 simulator was so impressive. It sat on three long hydraulic jacks, which suspended the whole platform a few feet in the air. Inside, the simulator was exactly like the airplane itself, and the visuals were so realistic.

The simulator session went well, and I was very happy that I had the chance to see everything before the simulator evaluation overseas. It allowed me to see what the cockpit of the 747 looked like, familiarize myself with the airplane's handling and power settings, experience a flight simulator, and mostly practice the flight profile.

747-400 flight simulator, Minneapolis, November 2005.

The airline provided flight tickets for all the Canadian candidates for the second stage of the interview. For the flight, I wore a suit, as I'd heard rumors that candidates were interviewed way before arriving overseas. We were told that we could be observed during boarding and even on the flight by the crew members who knew the candidates were on board. I can't confirm if that was true or just rumors, but the passengers sure looked at me funny for wearing a shirt and tie in the economy section for fourteen hours.

The airline had reservations for the candidates at their designated hotel, and I even received spending money during check-in. We were well taken care of, and I was really impressed by the airline.

Since I arrived early, I had a couple of days to see the city and get a feel for what it would be like to live in this part of the world. The city had a lot of places to explore, and I eagerly tried some local sushi restaurants. After a few days of exploring, I found that I would be very comfortable living overseas and pursuing my career outside Canada.

It's showtime—interview day.

For the second interview, the panel included the chief pilot and another management pilot. The interview was held in a big conference room. The panel was friendly but serious; I forced myself to remain calm and not get intimidated. It had been six months since the first invitation from the airline, and I knew this day would be the most important day—I had to shine.

The questions were very technical, as in the first interview. I felt I answered most of them well, with as much detail as I could, but there were a couple of meteorology questions where I was asked for more explanation and examples. No matter how much you prepare, you just can't know everything.

They asked me about my thoughts on moving and working in a new country and the challenges I would be faced with, hence the reason I arrived overseas a few days in advance—to get familiar with and learn about the new place I could potentially be living in. The interview lasted approximately forty-five minutes. I stepped out of the conference room, stopped in the hallway by the elevator, and thought to myself how badly I wanted the job and hoped I did well. I didn't have much time before I had to head to the simulator center for my evaluation. After a quick bathroom break, I went to another building where all the airline's simulators were; I wished I had time for a bite and to relax between the back-to-back evaluations.

As I walked to the simulator center, I went over everything I had practiced in the simulator in Minneapolis one last time in my head. I was greeted by two check pilots and received a pre-sim briefing before we headed to the simulator. I had to quickly switch my mind from interview mode to flying mode. I couldn't afford to think and analyze my performance in the interview, going over how I did or if there were answers I messed up. Just like on a PPC or a line check, if you make a mistake or don't know something perfectly, move on—don't overthink or analyze because the battle is not over. I had to stay focused for this next evaluation.

The session went by quickly, and within twenty-five minutes we were done. I'm sure glad I did the simulator session in Minneapolis. It would have been overwhelming to get in the simulator for the first time during an interview process without ever being in a 747 cockpit.

The next day, we had a group exercise with people from HR observing our teamwork, personalities, and decision-making processes as individuals and as a group. In the group exercise, we elected one team leader to write our ideas on the board. We were seven in my group, all with different flying experiences. Some flew corporate jets, and other turboprops. Three of us were Canadians—two from Winnipeg, one was an American, and the rest were European. We were a great bunch of guys and made good friendships right away.

Our exercise was to select the right individuals from a stack of résumés to be trained as astronauts to embark on a space mission. There were no right or wrong professionals to choose; the goal was for HR personnel to watch us work together as a team, evaluate us individually, and get to know us better.

That evening, the whole group went out for dinner. It was a nice way to release the stress and the pressure of the interview process and just to have a relaxing time.

The next day, I had to complete a very thorough medical exam, lasting a few hours, as everything from head to toe was examined. After that, I headed back to the hotel and spent the rest of the day relaxing by the pool.

The last and final stage of the interview was a cocktail party with management, which was just as important as the interview itself. It was an opportunity for the airline's personnel to spend time with the candidates and their spouses in a social environment. The two pilots who interviewed me were there as well. For some reason, I felt I was still being interviewed by them.

I used the next day to pack and get ready for the return flight back to Canada. After finally finishing the interview process, I felt like a huge heavy load was removed from my shoulders. It had been a long six months of preparation; now it was all done and a matter of waiting for the outcome.

The flight back to Vancouver and then Winnipeg was long, and all I had on my mind was the interview process and my performance. I enjoyed being overseas and was looking forward to flying for that airline, even more so after the process.

I was happy to get back to work and fly again so that I could put my mind off the experience. We were told to wait two weeks before calling HR to find out if the interview process was successful and for a hiring date. Those two weeks felt like an eternity. Every day was dragging slowly. For a pilot or anyone who's been through an interview process, waiting for the outcome is always hard. No matter how much you try to keep yourself busy, it's always on your mind.

It was a late Sunday evening, and I just walked into the training department office after giving a training flight. It was the day I had to call the airline for my interview result. I briefed the pilot I was training that evening, finished all the paperwork, and just waited in the office for a couple of hours until it was 9:30 a.m. overseas to call the airline's Human Resources department. I wanted to be alone when I called and not home. I figured if the result was positive, I would scream from joy, and if negative, at least I would be alone for a few minutes to digest everything.

There are moments in our lives that would stay in our memories forever. We would not forget the moment, where we were, and how we felt. This day was one of them, and I remember every detail of that evening as if it was yesterday.

As I was dialing the number, I could feel my heart beating faster and faster. The phone rang three times, and I was transferred to a voicemail of the person I had to contact for the result. I waited another long and stressful thirty minutes, and then called back again.

I was able to reach HR on the second try. The lady from HR sounded happy on the phone and asked for my applicant number and my name. I was somehow relieved when I heard her happy voice. I figured if I wasn't successful, then she would have been more serious. She told me to wait for a few seconds while she was searching for my file. At that point, I could feel my heartbeat in my throat. I knew whatever result I heard would change my life and career path forever. I had a hard time holding the phone in my hand; for a moment I wished there was a better way to find out an interview result. Maybe an email would have been much easier, as this was nerve-racking.

A few seconds after being on hold, she was back, "Unfortunately, Mr. Mofet, you were not selected."

It took some time for those words to sink in. I felt my body temperature increasing suddenly, and the shock was slowly kicking in. I was searching for words but felt as if I was frozen and couldn't say anything. I composed myself and asked again if this result was for me by repeating my candidate number and my name, but unfortunately it was confirmed that yes, it was for me.

There was nothing else she could have told me, and she thanked me for applying. I thanked her as well, said that I wished the outcome was positive as I really wanted the job, and that I would reapply.

I hung up the phone and just sat there in the training room for hours with tears in my eyes. I wished that moment wasn't real and was instead just a nightmare, that I would wake up shortly from it all. But it was real and I had to accept it. I was devastated. I just couldn't believe this was really happening. I gave 100% dedication and six months of my life for that interview process. I wondered to myself what went wrong and why I wasn't selected. This was the first time I felt I didn't succeed in something, and it was hurtful to accept.

I learned early in my career that this profession has ups and downs, highs and lows. It has periods where everything's going well, positive things are happening, and you are moving forward and succeeding, but then it has periods where nothing is going your way, no matter the effort or sacrifices.

Today, looking back, I realize that things always seem to turn around and be positive in the end. Although it was hard to accept the fact I wasn't selected, I realized that some things happen for a reason. I had learned a great deal during those six months of preparing for that interview, and I knew this newfound knowledge would not go to waste but benefit me for the rest of my career and my future. There were other great airlines that were hiring—it was time to look elsewhere.

MY FRIEND CHRIS IRESON

When I had gotten the invite to my first stage interview in San Francisco, I called one of my close friends and colleagues who had been interviewed by the airline before. I wanted to get his insight into the interview process. We got together one Sunday afternoon, and Chris helped me prepare.

Chris was hired by Perimeter a few years after I got on with the airline, and we became friends right away. He was one of the brightest men I had ever met, talented, and had the most amazing sense of humor. Music, flying, and travel were his passions. We could talk for hours about airplanes.

One day, a group of us were in the airline's hangar just talking and catching up before heading on our separate flights, when suddenly we noticed a girl wearing a mechanic's jumpsuit, working on an airplane's instruments. I could see Chris's eyes light up when he first saw her. She was pretty and something about the fact she worked on an airplane made her even more attractive. Chris looked at me and said that someday, he was going to date her and that she would be his girlfriend. We laughed and started bugging Chris that he had no chance, and he replied to us, "You boys just watch." Chris proved us all wrong.

Chris and Kourtenay got married a few years later. She made his life complete; he had found bliss in the "State of Kourtenay." They had a beautiful wedding in Toronto, which I attended.

We both got hired with a regional airline in Toronto a few months apart in 2006. I was in Montreal, going through simulator training, when I received an email from a friend that Chris was diagnosed with terminal cancer. He fought a courageous and long battle. I visited Chris often when I used to travel back to Winnipeg. I was always so happy to see him but, at the same time, sad and devasted to see my friend suffer.

Chris taught me to enjoy life, not to take things too seriously, and that love is the greatest feeling to have. Flying and aviation are amazing, but there's no need to devote your entire life and effort only to work; you've got to dedicate time to yourself and your loved ones.

Chris passed away on September 6, 2007, but he lives on in our lives through great memories and stories. His laugh and beautiful soul will forever be missed. "Okey!"

LEAVING WINNIPEG

Following the news I received from the interview overseas, I decided that I would continue to pursue other airlines. I enjoyed working at Perimeter and with my coworkers there; the flying was a rewarding, fun, and challenging experience, but it was time to move on. By providing safe flying, good customer service, and most of all quality instructing and teaching, I believe I accomplished my mission of giving back to the airline that gave me my first opportunity in the industry. I was able to share my knowledge with the company pilots and be part of maintaining a successful training department. It was time to grow as a pilot, fly a jet airplane, and move to a different city.

I was invited to an interview with a big regional airline in Toronto not long after applying with them. By that time, I had accumulated a solid captain flight experience, which was well above the minimum required to apply.

I arrived in Toronto a day before my interview and stayed with a friend whom I met overseas, as we were both going through the interview process. I was interviewed by the chief pilot and an HR representative. Both were very pleasant to interview with and made me feel part of the team right away. It was relaxing and straightforward; overall, it went very well. I was later called for a simulator evaluation.

I received a call from HR a few days after the simulator evaluation and was officially hired. My start date was March 2006; I was to report to orientation week in Toronto. Nine years after starting flight school and six years after being hired at Perimeter, here I was getting ready for a new adventure, a new airline, a new airplane, a new city, and new challenges.

Perimeter Aviation and the city of Winnipeg gave me a lot in life, and I am forever grateful. Perimeter and its employees were like a family. I was fortunate to fly seven years up to Northern Manitoba and Ontario, which was an incredible and rewarding experience. I was lucky to work and fly with talented pilots. During my time with

Perimeter, I met and made amazing friendships with First Nations people as well. The chance that I had to serve their communities and to see beautiful places in our Northern Canada was wonderful.

I loaded my Honda Civic sedan with one suitcase and my flight bag and was ready to hit the road to Toronto, where I'd be living. I took as little as I could with me, as I initially planned to stay at a hotel once arriving in the city.

★   ★   ★

I will end this chapter with a memorable story that happened to me while I lived in Winnipeg.

My younger brother, Nir, came for a visit to Winnipeg to join me to go see one of our favorite rock bands in concert: Metallica.

On the morning of the concert, while having breakfast, my brother came up with the idea to go see if we could find out the hotel the band was staying at to perhaps have a chance to meet them. Now, since Winnipeg is a relatively small city, we decided to go visit a couple of major hotels in downtown Winnipeg, with the hopes of bumping into one of the band members.

This was perhaps not the best idea, but we had the whole day to kill, so we figured we had nothing to lose. My brother brought with him his Garage Inc. vinyl album, a compilation of cover songs by the band, just in case we would meet any band members. We visited a couple big hotels in the city but did not see the heavy metal band at any of them, so we decided to drop our silly plan and go catch an afternoon movie—*Kill Bill*—by our favorite movie director, Quentin Tarantino.

We walked into the Polo Park mall movie theatre, about fifteen to twenty minutes before the show started, and grabbed seats just below the middle of the theatre. It was a beautiful summer afternoon, so the movie theatre was nearly empty, with maybe ten or so people scattered about.

The movie was amazing, and once it ended, I remained seated to read the movie credits, as I was curious to know the name of an actor that played in the movie. My brother, on the other hand, stood up, telling me something fast and quietly, but I couldn't understand him.

"Hang on a sec. I'm reading the credits," I replied to him, but he again quickly said something to me. This time I looked at him, confused, trying to understand what the hell he was telling me.

He got his face right next to my nose and said, "James Hetfield is right behind us. I'm going to get the vinyl from the car. Don't let him leave." Then he vanished.

My jaw dropped as soon as I saw him. I was in shock. What were the chances that we'd see a movie, in Winnipeg, on the day of a Metallica concert, with James Hetfield, the lead singer of Metallica, sitting a row behind us? I said hi, and after a nod from his bodyguard I extended my hand for a handshake. I told James how much his music meant to me and my brother while my brother sprinted to the car to get his vinyl. He returned within what seemed like five seconds and had James sign his album.

There we were, looking for Metallica in hotels downtown the whole afternoon, while the man himself, the leader of the band, was there right next to us.

Maybe it's a life lesson: sometimes the things we chase might just come to us on their own when least expected!

CHAPTER 6

✈

(YYZ)

While driving to Toronto, I thought about my life and career to this point. I'd been to Toronto a few times in the past to visit, but now I was going to live there. It would be a new beginning—learning about the city, making new friends, and finding a place to live. As far as my career, at that point I had flown the same airplane for seven years and was accustomed to the same procedures. This comfort had given me great confidence—I was ready to embark on a new journey. I was ready to learn to fly a new airplane and learn new company procedures. This was also my first time leaving an airline for another one, and it was going to take time to feel that comfort again. I knew there would be new challenges ahead, but my bag of tools and the knowledge I had accumulated from the last seven years would help me; I hoped.

Arriving in Toronto, I was reminded of how big the city is, and the size of the highways took some getting used to as well. The iPhone didn't exist at that time. Before going anywhere in the city, I looked at a map and then drew my route on a piece of paper so as not to get lost. Eventually, I got used to the highway system and the route structure.

I was staying at a hotel right next to Toronto Pearson International Airport for orientation week, which lasted five days. I arrived at the hotel Saturday night and took Sunday as a day to prepare myself for the week. I unpacked, ironed all my shirts, and prepared my flight bag.

The first day of the orientation week went well. We were in a big classroom, sitting in three rows. I was impressed with the airline and the people from various departments that came to talk to us. We were a group of seventeen pilots, all coming from different airlines and cities, all with different experiences and backgrounds. We had a chance to introduce ourselves and talk about what kind of flying we did at the previous airlines we worked for.

I was looking forward to the third day of the orientation week, as we were going to find out what base and airplane we would be assigned to. The base was not that important to me, as I didn't have a permanent place to live anyway. What I really wanted to know was the type of airplane I would be assigned to. The airline had the Bombardier Canadair regional jets (CRJ 100/200/705) and the De Havilland Dash-8 turboprop aircraft—I wanted to fly the jet. To fly at higher altitudes, into busy airports, and with more advanced technology would be a great experience for me.

The number of jets, turboprops airplanes, or bases available for the group varied from one ground school to the other. Some ground schools had all jets, and others all turboprops. Some had all bases in YYZ, and some were mixed.

When the afternoon of the third day came around, the chief pilot walked into the classroom and spoke to us about the operations and the company. He seemed very nice and I was looking forward to flying with him. The union rep eventually joined him as well, and on a board, he wrote the number of airplanes and bases available for our group to choose from.

Eight RJ jets were available, all based in YYZ, and nine Dash-8 turboprops, at a mix of bases between YYZ and YUL.

The airplane and base assigned for each pilot was simply randomly chosen. We all wrote our names on a business card, which was then put in the chief pilot's hat. The union rep pulled one card at a time, and once your name was called, you were able to choose the airplane/ base of your choice, depending on what was left.

For me, that was the most intense moment of the week. Wherever I was going to be based would be the city I would move to. Also, the type of airplane I would be assigned to would determine the type of flying and lifestyle I would have. If I was assigned to a jet, I would have longer flights with fewer takeoffs and landings versus the turboprop, as well as more US destinations. It would also be a great way to see other cities and have layovers.

The cards were coming out and every person was taking the RJ jet in Toronto base—obviously!

The fourth, the fifth, the sixth cards were coming out, but none were mine, and slowly the jet spots were reduced. I was becoming more and more discouraged until I noticed something strange: the cards were coming out in the same order we were sitting in. The first cards picked were of all those sitting in the front row of the classroom. It appeared to me that the cards were not shuffled well, and since the cards of those sitting in the front of the class were put in the hat last, they were the ones coming out first, which meant my card was somewhere stacked in the middle, as I was sitting in the second row and mid-section of the classroom.

Something had to be done and fast; otherwise, I was about to end up not flying a jet.

"I think we should shuffle the cards better," I said out loud.

Card number eight was pulled, and it wasn't my name. *There goes the last jet airplane for the class,* I thought. But when the name of the eighth pilot was called, he chose the Dash-8 aircraft since he wanted to be based in YUL. That meant there was one jet left for grabs—who would be the lucky guy? Me! The next card had my name on it. I was so happy, I almost jumped off my seat.

The rest of the week went very well, and I was paired up for simulator training with a nice fellow from the West Coast. We became good friends and spent a lot of time together during our training. My simulator partner had a great sense of humor; we went out during our free time and our favorite meal was sushi.

We found this little sushi restaurant on Bloor Street, in downtown Toronto, that advertised all-you-can-eat sushi for $14.95. We ordered a salad each and a huge number of salmon and tuna sashimi; I think the restaurant lost money that day because of us. We returned a week later, and as we walked in, the chef wasn't happy to see us. The restaurant eventually brought up the price for the all-you-can-eat deal.

I had to look for a place to live in Toronto, as I was now based there. For the first couple of months, I rented a room in a large three-bedroom condo with two other colleague pilots from the airline. Going from owning a home in Winnipeg to living with roommates was a big change for me, but I enjoyed staying there for the month; it felt like living on a college campus.

Simulator training was at full force, and we were enjoying learning the CRJ airplane. First, we learned about the aircraft's systems through an online training program. As long as deadlines were met, we were able to study and complete the modules at our own pace. The simulator sessions were built in a way to introduce malfunctions and failures step-by-step, with every session starting simple at the beginning, then becoming more challenging as they progressed. The training program was top-notch.

Towards the end of the simulator program, we were invited to the hangar to learn how to perform a pre-flight walk-around. Although the cockpit was exactly like inside the simulator, when I first walked into it I was so excited; I couldn't wait to fly the airplane. The cockpit looked cool, and once I sat in it, I was able to see the height change from the Metro. It was exhilarating—the thought of flying a jet was soon becoming a reality.

June 3, 2006 was our last simulator session on the RJ705, and we had the opportunity to practice touch-and-go landings. We accumulated forty-eight hours of simulator training before my first official flight on June 11, 2006, which was from Toronto (YYZ) to Thunder Bay (YQT) on RJ100 aircraft. June 12, 1997 was the first time I flew the Cessna 152 airplane as a student, and here I was, nine years later, flying a jet aircraft. What a great feeling!

I arrived at the crew room located at Pearson International, Terminal 1. Working for such a big airline and being new, it took some time to find the captain I was flying with. We went through the flight paperwork and headed to the airplane to do a walk-around. Once that was done, we returned to the cockpit and continued with the pre-flight preparation.

The beauty of airline flying is that what you learn and can do in the simulator, you apply on the line. The difference is now you have real passengers behind you and not an instructor.

After many years of turboprop flying, the first time flying a jet was an unbelievable experience. The first thing you notice is how much quieter the airplane is without the loud propellers. Also, the engines on the RJ are way in the back of the airplane, so the flight deck is a quiet and peaceful environment to work in.

The first few flights on the RJ were line training flights, where I familiarized myself with the company route sector and reviewed drills and systems and many other topics. My line check was completed on July 1 on the RJ 705, which is the longer version of the RJ 100 model and also had a first-class cabin. A line check flight is a normal revenue flight with passengers, but includes a check pilot, who observes, assesses, and grades the pilot's performance during various stages of the flight. The pilot must also review selected drills and memory items to confirm their knowledge and overall performance. This line check was the final part of my RJ training, and I was released from training, which lasted two months altogether.

FLYING A JET FOR THE FIRST TIME AND PREP FOR A NEW TYPE RATING

The CRJ jet is an amazing airplane to fly and a great transition jet-airplane from a turboprop. On the other hand, what I had to get used to was the loss of the engine noise during power changes. On a turboprop, it's obvious, but not on the CRJ. Also, the biggest difference is, of course, the takeoff and approach speeds, which were much higher on the CRJ. Since the CRJ is an airplane with swept-back wings, it takes some time for the airplane to decelerate from the 320 knots descent speed to 250 knots, which is the maximum speed below 10,000 feet. Therefore, a pilot must plan and monitor its descent profile to meet all altitude and speed restrictions and not to get caught too high and fast.

When flying jets, you learn that it takes some time for the airplane to slow down while on your descent. If a pilot wants to expedite a descent, for example, and slow down, they can't do it simultaneously. One technique is to expedite down to a lower altitude and then, once leveled, slow down. Another option is to decelerate first, then descend, which could leave a pilot high on the descent profile. These techniques are executed by using different autopilot vertical modes during the descent, which are essential to learning early during line training. Understanding the various flight management modes that control the autopilot, flight director (FD), and the autothrust system is important. That is fundamental, and the earlier the pilot masters the usage of these modes, the easier the line flying will be, and of course it's a better way to manage the flight. The autopilot modes might be named differently from one aircraft manufacturer to the other, but the concept remains the same and these techniques could be used whether flying an Airbus, a Boeing, or any other aircraft manufacturer.

The autopilot control panel of the Airbus A321 Full Flight Simulator.

On the descent, it is always good to compare your distance and altitude to ensure you are not high on your descent profile. The 3 to 1 rule works best—3 nautical miles of travel should be allowed for every 1,000 feet of descent. If you are at 30,000 feet on the descent and on speed, your distance should be at least 90 nautical miles from the runway. The flight management system (FMS) will ensure the correct profile will be maintained if descending in Manage Mode (Airbus) or VNAV mode (Boeing) but being aware of this basic formula will ensure you don't end up too high on descent. Also, in case being kept high by Air Traffic Control, for an example, knowing how to return back on profile is important as well.

Additional use of this rule-of-thumb is on the final approach, which generally has a 3-degree vertical angle. This corresponds to 3 nautical miles (nm) per 1000 feet, which again makes mental estimation simple.

Here are some pointers on how to prepare yourself for training on a new type of aircraft. First, if the training includes online technical training, complete that as soon as possible. You want to get that out of the way first so you can focus on studying aircraft procedures. Second, it is important to read the airplane's standard operating procedures (SOPs) at least a couple of times. You need to speak the same "language"; therefore, this manual is vital. Once that is complete, review all drills, memory items, and flows so it will be performed easily in the simulator from memory. Some airlines will provide posters of the cockpit panels or a software.

Then reviewing all simulator syllabi will prepare you for the exercises that will be performed in the simulator. You don't want to be surprised in training; you want to have seen or read the checklists beforehand that will be used with these malfunctions. Once all the simulator sessions are completed, a good review of all drills and memory items and the SOPs will be beneficial before the final simulator test.

For line training, a good review of the company procedures or operations manual will be important before the first flight. Also, all drills will need to be reviewed since these will be asked about during the training and final line check.

Time management is key when learning a new airplane type, therefore putting a couple of months off for strictly studying and preparation is important for an enjoyable and successful training.

With the RJ jet, we mostly flew into very busy airspaces and big airports in the United States. It was an excellent experience dealing with holding clearances, challenging taxi clearances, and being proficient with the FMS programming. An FMS is a fundamental component of a modern airliner's avionics. An FMS is a specialized computer system that automates a wide variety of in-flight tasks. Using various sensors in the aircraft (such as GPS and Inertial navigation System (INS) often backed up by radio navigation) to determine the aircraft's position, the FMS can also guide the aircraft using the programmed flight plan with the usage of the autopilot, Flight Director, and autothrust systems. Programing the FMS will enable you to perform an ILS approach with Autoland where the aircraft will perform the approach and landing automatically from the cockpit, the FMS is normally controlled through a control display unit (CDU), which incorporates a small screen and keyboard or touchscreen.

A321 NEO FMS/CDU (Greenland can be seen ahead to the right)

★   ★   ★

We were on a regularly scheduled flight enroute from YYZ to LaGuardia New York (LGA) when we experienced a dual FMS failure during the descent and the arrival. The FMS system had the programmed arrival flight plan, where the aircraft was following and guiding the aircraft automatically. With that failure, both autopilots disconnected and the captain who was the "pilot flying" had to hand-fly the aircraft, which is not a difficult task. The navigation part was the issue, as now we had no guidance information available to our navigation display unit.

Trying to put a word through to Air Traffic Control in such busy airspace was a challenge, but I managed to jump on the frequency and inform the controller of the problem. The controller, who was extremely busy at that time with many airplanes under his control, ordered us to follow a few landmarks until he was able to get back to us with radar vectors to the final approach.

My job was to help the captain navigate since all he could do was fly the airplane—which is the number one thing to do. We eventually received radar vectors and landed the aircraft with no other issues. The whole flight was nice and relaxing until the last fifteen minutes.

The difference between the flight simulator, where all training is done, versus real life is that things can and will happen when least expected. Therefore, no matter what happens, fly the airplane first!

THIRTY-ONE YEARS OLD— THE HIGHS AND LOWS

Flying for the regional airline was very enjoyable and rewarding, and it was a great company to work for. I was treated well and working conditions were excellent. I learned a lot and became comfortable with the airplane and the routes. After training was completed, my schedule reverted to a reserve block, so I was mostly on call. Basically, I was sitting and waiting. The reserve schedule is unpredictable since you never know when you'll get called. You must plan your day accordingly and be ready to head to the airport for a crew pairing lasting a day or up to five.

Living in Toronto was amazing; I fell in love with the city and what it had to offer. Toronto is a modern, multi-cultural city with a lively nightlife, friendly people, lots of things to do, and great weather. Also, I was closer to Montreal and was able to see my family a lot more often than when I lived in Winnipeg.

After a month of living in the condo with my pilot colleagues, I had to move out and find a cheaper place. I had taken a salary cut when I left Winnipeg and was now making just under $35,000 a year. The salary with the new airline was known to me from the start, and I knew that I would have to adjust my lifestyle moving to Toronto. When a pilot changes companies, they will have to be ready to take a pay reduction and start at the bottom of the seniority list. That will also affect many other things, such as schedules and other bidding options. All of this occurs in almost all airlines.

If making lots of money or becoming a millionaire is the key goal for someone, then pursuing a pilot career might not be the best choice. In my opinion, pilots in Canada are generally underpaid when they are newly hired with an airline. The responsibilities required to take on every flight, their knowledge and skill, the countless hours of studying, constant testing/evaluations, and the sacrifices made are not rewarded early in a pilot's career. But on a good note, once a pilot remains with an airline for a good number of years, salaries do go up and pilots can eventually make a very comfortable living.

While I was searching for a cheaper place to live, I heard from a colleague about some "crash pads" that were available by the airport, and the place lived up to its name—it was a pad you could crash in.

Usually, these are two- or three-bedroom apartments with bunk beds close to the airport that provide commuting pilots and flight attendants a place to stay before or after a flight rotation. If you are based in YYZ and commute, you can arrive at the crash pad the day before a pairing rotation and leave the next day for a flight. Although convenient and very cheap, there is nothing glamorous about these apartments. Some pads can be nicer than others, but I paid $140 per month, which wasn't expensive at that time.

At the crash pad where I stayed, ten pilots were renting the place. On average, we were two to five in the two-bedroom and one bathroom apartment at the same time. The building was old and not in the safest neighborhood. We had two bunk beds and a closet in one room; the second room had one bunk bed and one double bed.

My bed is the one with the paper sign: "Gerry's bed."

Most people who used the crash pad would come and go, but I made that place a permanent home for nine months. My plan was to save money to eventually buy a condo. When I had just moved into the crash pad, my mom came from Montreal for a visit. I could see her disappointment when she first saw the apartment I was living in. She knew about all the sacrifices I had made in my career and had hoped I would be living in a better place after all these years in aviation.

A typical reserve day would start with our cell phones ringing between 5:00 and 6:00 a.m. With three pilots in the same room, sleeping in was not an option during that time. The night before, you needed to have your uniform ready so that you didn't wake everyone up as you got ready for a flight.

One evening, four of us were in our crash pad, sitting on the old couch we'd found in the dumpster, watching a hockey game between the Toronto Maple Leafs and the Montreal Canadiens. One of my roommates said, "Hey, guys, we made it!" We all laughed so hard. Where we were wasn't glamorous, but you had to laugh about it.

Like in many other professions, sacrifices are required to advance and to succeed. We need to give to gain.

★   ★   ★

Approximately six months after getting hired with the airline and being comfortable on the RJ, I contacted my good friend Ron at Perimeter, who was the training manager on the Metro airplane. I asked if he needed any help in the training department, and he happily accepted having me come back to Perimeter on a part-time basis to help as an instructor.

With the approval of the chief pilot at my current airline, I was able to work part-time for Perimeter, training on the Metro just like I did before I left.

Teaching is something I've always enjoyed. I had a lot of experience on the Metro and felt I still had a lot to offer to the training department and Perimeter's pilots. It was a lot of work to be proficient on both airplanes, and time management was important.

I was able to make a little more money so I could eventually leave the crash pad and purchase my first condo, which I did at the beginning of 2007. It felt great to finally become a condo owner and not have roommates anymore.

Seven months after starting with the airline, I was able to hold a block schedule and stopped being on reserve. I could finally stop staring at my phone all the time. I was able to get more flights on the newer CRJ 705 and enjoyed the nice layovers we had in the United States.

I had a rewarding and fun flying experience with the airline. I flew with great pilots and made amazing friendships. There were excellent benefits, and one of them was the travel opportunities. I had the chance to travel to beautiful places, such as LA, New York, Hawaii, and Australia to name a few.

If you are passionate about travel, culture, working with enthusiastic and fun people, and seeing and discovering the world, then airline flying is the way to go.

As the flying experience grew so did the opportunities that came with it, which brought me to another airline.

EVERYTHING HAPPENS FOR A REASON

I met Luc in flight college in 1997, and we became friends right away. We stayed in touch after graduating, even though we both took different paths in our search for our first pilot job. I ended up in Winnipeg, whereas Luc headed overseas.

When we were both at the flight college, a pilot from Air Transat came to talk to us about the airline and his career progression. We were both inspired by that airline, and Luc said that Air Transat was going to be the airline he would like to fly for someday. I shared the same feelings, as I had the opportunity to travel with the airline in the past and was always inspired by the airline's culture, the type of flying they did, and the airplanes they operated.

Air Transat had not hired for a while and even had layoffs in 2003–2004. Hiring started in 2006, and the airline had interviews almost every month.

When Luc was hired with Air Transat, he offered to bring my résumé to HR, which I was very grateful for. No one had ever offered to do that for me before, and I was happy for the opportunity despite applying for many years and never receiving a call for an interview.

When Air Transat called me to schedule the interview, I thought it was a prank call from a friend or just a joke—I couldn't believe they called me. When I became captain at Perimeter in 2001, I used to send résumés to Air Transat every six months as I was accumulating flight hours. I never received a reply from the airline, so when I received the call I was very excited.

At this point in my career, I had a solid flight experience. I was thirty-one, with over 7000 hours total flight time, with the majority as pilot-in-command, I had airline jet and training pilot experience, and I was fully bilingual.

I started preparing for my interview by researching about the airline's history, corporate culture, mission statement, key personnel, route structure, and sales history, and by preparing for the simulator evaluation on the Airbus A310.

The interview process at that time was done in the following order: an interview at the head office in Montreal, a simulator evaluation, and lastly, a medical exam.

I reviewed all the standard and possible interview questions I could expect to be asked. I ordered a cockpit DVD video by Royal Airlines on the A310. It was filmed during a flight from Toronto to Glasgow and was a great way to familiarize myself with the cockpit switches and panel layout. I also got some pictures and posters of the A310 cockpit.

When I got called for the interview, I had almost eight years of airline flying under my belt. Therefore, to help me prepare I looked back at my career and recalled all the events and experiences I'd been through—how I got to where I was, what I had seen and learned in those eight years, the good decisions I'd made, and how I learned from my mistakes. I also thought about where I saw myself in the future, what else I'd like to learn, and how I would like to advance in my profession. I self-analyzed myself so that I would be able to talk about my experience and what I could bring to the airline as a pilot and employee. By doing that, I was able to prepare answers to almost any question I could be asked because I had examples to share with my answers.

I arrived the night before the interview and stayed at my mom's house in Montreal. My interview was scheduled at 10:00 a.m. at the airline's headquarters. I wore a blue suit like the airline's company colors. I parked my car three blocks away from the airline's office at 7:00 a.m. My plan was to head over to the headquarters at 9:40 a.m. If for whatever reason my car had not started, I was only fifteen minutes away. Being late for the interview was not an option!

I walked to the Air Transat Headquarters right at 9:45 a.m. and walked straight to the front desk. I smiled and introduced myself. The receptionist welcomed me and offered a seat, telling me that someone from HR would be with me soon. I was impressed with the building and felt positive while sitting and waiting to be called. Not long after, a lady from HR approached and introduced herself and invited me to follow her to the interview room. Inside the little room were two company captains, one of which was a supervisor and the other represented the pilot union. Both introduced themselves, and I gave them a solid handshake. I wasn't nervous being there; I actually felt comfortable despite the fact the supervisor seemed strict and wasn't smiling. The room I was interviewed in was very small compared to the one I was interviewed in overseas.

The lady from HR explained the interview process, and when I was asked the first question, I replied by first thanking everyone for the opportunity and for their time to interview me. The rest of the questions were straightforward, and the interview moved on steadily. My favorite question was about my entire aviation career, from the beginning until now. I believe the answer to the question was the highlight of the interview. I was able to share my story and about my move to Winnipeg, how I used to go see Mark every two weeks for seven months so that he would hire me, and about the rest of my career progression. After answering that question, I felt the positive energy and the connection with the interviewers. I even managed to make the supervisor smile.

At the end of the interview, I thanked the panel again, and when asked if I had any questions for them, I answered that I didn't at that moment. Some recommend having a question or two prepared for the interview panel to show interest, but in my opinion it's not necessary.

We shook hands, and I was asked to wait by the waiting area. Ten minutes later, I was greeted by the operations manager, who asked me to follow him to his office on the second floor at Flight Operations. I figured the fact I was meeting him was a good sign, but I didn't let overconfidence take over. The interview wasn't over, and I knew this stage was very important.

He asked me a few basic questions about myself, why I wanted to work for the airline, and why I should be selected. He was impressed with my flight experience, and I felt we had a good conversation.

I was then sent to the simulator training center for the simulator evaluation. It was a ten-minute drive to get to the center. I believe that the simulator evaluation can count for a great deal in the final evaluation of a candidate in many airlines. It may not be the make it or break it part of the interview process, as the airline is aware that some candidates may never have flown the Airbus A310 or other types used in the evaluation, but regardless, many important things are evaluated in that session: hand-flying skills, IFR knowledge, CRM, and to see if the candidate is trainable. The interview is a way to get to know the candidate and see if they are a good fit with the airline culture. On the other hand, the simulator evaluation is to evaluate the kind of pilot the candidate is.

In the simulator, the cockpit layout, switches, knobs, flight instruments, and controls are just like the airplane. The simulator stands on three hydraulic jacks, which move as the pilot makes control inputs on the wheel or as the autopilot makes flight changes. The only thing a simulator cannot simulate is the pressure change we feel in our ears; otherwise, it's as real as it gets.

I checked in at the security desk in the simulator center and headed upstairs to the second floor, where the waiting lounge was. I noticed another candidate was already there. Pilots usually don't wear a suit and tie in the simulator center, so I figured he was there for the evaluation as well.

"Are you here for the 2:00 p.m. evaluation?" I asked.

We were going in the simulator together because two pilots were to be evaluated at the same time. As we waited, we chatted a little about the interview process and which airline we worked for. Not long after, we met with the supervisor pilots who would evaluate us in the simulator.

"Who wants to go first?" one of the supervisors asked.

"I'll go first," I replied.

I had jet experience and more flight experience than the other candidate, so I figured I'd go first, and the other candidate would be able to watch my session from the jumpseat.

From the outside, the Airbus A310 simulator didn't look as sophisticated compared to the other aircraft simulators on the same floor. It looked like a big metal container, whereas the other sims looked a lot more futuristic. We walked into the simulator, and I sat in the first officer (FO) seat and strapped myself in with the five strap seatbelts. For a second, a flashback from the B747 simulator came to mind. I was thinking to myself how much calmer I felt this time; I didn't feel the same pressure to succeed as when I was overseas. I didn't rent simulator time before this evaluation, but because I flew the RJ jet I had the confidence and knowledge to face this evaluation.

I was sure glad I had looked at all the cockpit panels beforehand, as the A310 has very different instrumentation layout. One of the supervisors sat in the captain's seat, and the other supervisor sat at the instructor station. The other candidate sat in the jumpseat between the captain and FO seats.

The supervisor went over all the switches and controls we would use in the session, and off we went with my takeoff briefing. This was it—time to demonstrate everything I had learned all those years earlier. Once airborne, we went over some airwork exercises, such as steep turns and instrument procedures. I found that the Airbus A310 flew very similarly to the Metroliner. It was all about trimming the airplane well and putting small control inputs.

It is interesting, but the bigger the airplane the lighter the flight controls feel, and there is no need for heavy control inputs. You can fly a 150-ton airplane with just a couple of fingers on the control column. The beauty of the Airbus A310 is that it has the standard control column just like the Metro airplane and isn't like the other Airbus types with the fly-by-wire technology, such as the Airbus A320/A330 types.

We then proceeded for radar vectors for the non-precision approach. I was instructed to use the procedures and briefings used in my current airline and to fly the A310 approach profile, just as I would do on the CRJ. The session up until now had been going well.

Once established on the final approach, breaking out of the overcast cloud layer and with visual contact with the runway, I realized I was a little high, which wasn't good. Being high on a heavy jet makes it very hard to get back on the correct profile.

"Standby for possible go-around!" I informed the supervisor sitting on my left.

I decided to wait a few more seconds before initiating the go-around, hoping the small corrections during the final descent would put me back on profile.

"Go-around!" I called out and pitched the aircraft to fifteen degrees nose up and set takeoff/go-around (TOGA) thrust.

The aim of the exercise was to land, or at least be positioned for landing, but the safest course of action for me was to go around and not push the airplane to a steep descent. I would rather come back for a second, safer approach.

I flew the published missed approach and leveled the airplane at 3000 feet.

"Ok thanks, Gerry. The session is over. You can swap seats now," the supervisor running the session said and repositioned the airplane back on the ground.

My session had lasted twenty-five minutes, but it felt like only five had gone by.

Once the second candidate completed his turn, we were told there would be no debriefing and that HR would contact us within two weeks. We both thanked the supervisors, and on our way out of the training center, we exchanged phone numbers to call each other as soon as either of us heard from HR.

I went over the session in my head and analyzed my performance. I felt I did well overall, despite being high on final approach; I believed the decision to go around was good and hoped the instructors saw the same.

Waiting for airline job interview results can be very stressful. You'll likely go over your performance again and again, wondering if you did well enough to get hired.

It had been two weeks since the interview, and I hadn't heard anything from HR. No news is good news, I guess, but still I couldn't stop thinking about what the outcome would be.

August 3, 2007, I was on a layover, poolside in Atlanta, Georgia on a beautiful summer day when my cell phone rang. I got out of the pool and stared at the call display on my flip phone: area code 514 number. That's Montreal and it was a number not in my contacts. Who could that be?

"Mr. Mofet, we are happy to inform you that we would like to offer you a course start date for October 1," said the lady from HR.

The words were slowly sinking in my ears. I was ecstatic with joy. I was hired by one of the best airlines in the world, and I just couldn't be happier. It had been three weeks to the day since the interview.

That evening I invited the whole crew I was flying with, the captain and two flight attendants, for dinner at the Cheesecake Factory, my favorite restaurant chain in the United States. I was so happy, and there was no better way to celebrate such a special moment and good news with my crew.

CHAPTER 7

✈

When I walked through the main front doors at the Air Transat Headquarters—the same doors I walked through for my interview over a month ago—I met seven of my new colleagues as they were also walking into the building. Everyone had a solid flight experience from other airlines and from the military as well. I was looking forward to the next five days of orientation, to learn about the company structure and the training program.

During the next few days, we had people from HR, payroll, Flight Ops, and from the union come see us. Our seniority number was assigned depending on our experience, total time, and types of airplanes we have flown.

Seniority in a unionized airline is very important since many aspects take a pilot's seniority number into consideration. It will determine many things: schedule, vacation choices, and upgrading to a captain position to name a few.

That first day of orientation was very memorable to me. It had been a long journey, but I was finally hired at an airline I had always wanted to fly for. It seemed like everything led to this moment. Ten years had passed since taking my first flight lesson on the Cessna 152, and here I was, assigned to fly the 150-ton Airbus A310. I was excited about this new chapter in my life. I learned that sometimes things happen for a reason, and despite being disappointed in not succeeding overseas, this new chapter in my life was proof that great things come in life when you don't give up.

After orientation week was completed, we had a few days dedicated to completing all the online training. I planned to complete the online training quickly so that I could study the company SOPs, flows, memory items, and checklists. These are all very important to know well before simulator training begins. Initial training on a jetliner for a major airline takes approximately two months, and it requires a lot of dedication and time to succeed in the program.

In my studies, I realized that from one jet to another, the aircraft equipment is the same. For example, a generator, a hydraulic pump, or a fuel pump has the same function. The difference is how the equipment operates in the system. Airbus describes its different hydraulic systems on the aircraft by colors versus other manufacturer, which use A or B, or left or right, for example.

The A310 is considered a "heavy" aircraft in North America since it's capable of operating with a gross takeoff weight of more than 150 tons (300,000 lbs) and was used by the airline for overseas flights to Europe. I was looking forward to flying the aircraft and for oceanic operations.

I was paired up with another pilot from my class. Simulator training lasted just over a month and involved over a dozen training sessions. The sessions allowed us to go through many types of emergencies and to practice different types of approaches, such as ILS, non-precision approaches, GPS, and autoland approaches, where the airplane lands automatically via the autopilot system.

All these simulator sessions prepared the crew for the final test—the Pilot Proficiency Check (PPC)—which lasts four hours and is an opportunity for the check pilot to assess a pilot's proficiency with different malfunctions/failures and approaches. In our test, each one of us acted as a pilot flying and a pilot non-flying. Airline pilots go through these tests every six months to maintain proficiency and for the company to maintain a high level of pilot training and evaluation.

Airline pilots spend lots of time studying and preparing for continuous testing in their careers.

Our PPC Flight Test was on November 24, 2007, and we were officially type rated on the Airbus A310. It was a great achievement and feeling. We had over a week off before our touch-and-go training flight, so I planned a trip to New York City for the weekend off.

The touch-and-go landings training session was scheduled for December 4. This flight had to be completed before we started line indoctrination training. To pass this stage, each one of us had to complete three takeoffs and landings.

I had to deadhead (a North American term for repositioning) from Toronto to Montreal that morning since the training flight was departing from Montreal-Trudeau Airport.

While having breakfast the day of the flight and looking at my boarding pass, I was shocked to see that the boarding time was in thirty minutes. I was not sure if my flight had changed through Crew Scheduling during the week I had off. But regardless, I had to leave for the airport immediately or risk missing such an important training flight. Being late for my first flight would not look good with the airline.

Luckily I had packed my suitcase and flight bag the night before. I got dressed and was out the door in five minutes. Traffic on the 401 that morning did not help, and I made it to the flight with minutes to spare. You know those stressed people you see running in the terminal to the gate? That day I was that guy.

Once I arrived in Montreal, I headed straight to the crew room, where I met with the A310 supervisor and the rest of the pilot group, who were going to fly the touch-and-go landing training flight. It was nice to see the supervisor, as the last time I saw him was during my interview a few months before.

The supervisor briefed us about the flight. There would be a full cockpit preparation in YUL, push back and taxi to the active runway, take off from Montreal-Trudeau Airport, a short hop over to Mirabel Airport, then straight into the circuit pattern to perform three landings for each of us. Once each pilot performed their landing, we would swap seats and have the next pilot fly their approaches. We were five that day.

"Who's going first?" the supervisor asked.

Since we were departing YUL Airport, someone would have to be the FO on the departure from Montreal. No one volunteered.

"Gerry, you are going first," was the order. I was pumped and ready.

The cockpit preparation went well; we pushed back and departed to Mirabel. There was one thing I did not notice in the simulator that was noticeable right away in the airplane—the height at which I was sitting in the cockpit. In the cockpit of the A310, a pilot sits nineteen feet above ground, which is double the height from the CRJ aircraft.

Another thing I took a mental note of was that we were empty with no passengers on the flight, and with such low takeoff weight, the airplane would be airborne like a rocket. The General Electric CF6 engines were monstrous, with over 45,000 pounds of thrust each; therefore the climb was going to be quick and fast.

As we lined up on the runway in Montreal, I called, "Runway 24L, heading 237." Then I clicked the TOGA levers, which engaged the autothrust system, setting automatic takeoff power. The sound of the engines spooling up was magnificent, like a musical instrument. The sound had so much power because each engine was sucking all the air in front of it into its eighty-six-inch diameter huge front-engine fan.

The takeoff roll was quick, and the airplane was airborne, with slight back pressure on the control column. I leveled off and started to prepare to join the visual circuit into Mirabel Airport, which was a five-minute flight over. I lined up on the runway, all checks completed, then made small adjustments to keep center with the runway, maintaining speed and constant approach angle. I made hardly any changes on the thrust levers, as with such powerful engines, small thrust-lever movement produced all the thrust required to keep the approach speed.

Newton law: For every action, there is an equal and opposite reaction. Thrust forward, and the nose will go up; reduce thrust, and the opposite will happen. Relaxing is key—feel the airplane, make small corrections, and no overcontrolling.

Smooth landing, flaps up, trim set, and GO, we were airborne again. The next two landings went smoothly; once leveled, my colleague and I swapped seats and he was now at the controls. I left the cockpit and headed to the main cabin as another of my colleagues sat on the jumpseat.

All five of us had our turn to fly before we headed back to Montreal Airport. Fun day! Line indoctrination on live flights were next.

LINE INDOCTRINATION ON THE AIRBUS A310

I was thirty-two years old when I started flying at Air Transat, eight years after I had graduated from flight school. I had found my twenties challenging, a time when lots of hard work was required to get ahead. Those were years full of sacrifices. But although I had a low income and a lack of life experience and wisdom, I was full of desire and determination to achieve and succeed—I had no other choice. Learning was often done from mistakes, but I knew the key was not to repeat them.

In my early thirties, I finally started living life and enjoying the fruits of my success; there was no better place than being an airline pilot and flying all over the world.

The first flight of line indoctrination was on a revenue flight full of passengers from YUL to Cancun International Airport (CUN), on Airbus A310 C-GTSH (flight number TS682), on December 6, 2007—two months and a week after my first day of orientation week.

I had a special feeling as I walked in the passenger lounge and looked through the terminal glass window at the massive airplane parked on the ramp. I guess in every career that exciting moment exists: a doctor before performing a surgery, a journalist interviewing a celebrity, or a hockey player stepping on the ice before a game. The exciting feeling for a pilot happens right before a flight. After twenty-three years of flying, I still get that special feeling.

My training flights in the simulator involved constant failures and lots of approaches, landings, and takeoffs. But on that flight, I would feel a lot more relaxed. I was going to have the opportunity to operate the flight but also review the company procedures, drills, and malfunctions, and learn about the company's route structure.

On that flight we were full, with 250 passengers. The sound of the engines was as powerful and magical as it was in the touch-and-go training session, but this time I felt the weight of the airplane as the mighty beast was getting airborne.

It was an enjoyable flight, and for the first time I got to perform the cruise flow and checklist, as training in the simulator was mostly done at low altitude. We reviewed the aircraft's systems, operational company procedures, performance calculations, and weight and balance calculations, and started looking at the standard terminal arrival (STAR) and approach we were planning to fly into Cancun, Mexico.

Since my line training flights started in the winter, most of the flights I was assigned to were what we call in the industry "turns," meaning a flight originating in Canada would fly to the sunny southern Caribbean destinations and return to Canada the same day. The average flight would be four to five hours each leg, plus an hour and a half stopover. Since they were two-leg flights, I had the opportunity to land the airplane often. And once parked at the gate down south, us pilots had to recalculate the outbound weight and balance, program the return flight plan in the navigation system, and get ready for boarding. It was going to be a busy day.

After almost forty hours of line flight training, I was scheduled for my line check flight test on December 27, a turn from YUL to CCC Airport in Cuba. For me, it was going to be a straightforward flight, and I had a few days after the last line training flight to review and prepare myself. Pilots just never stop studying and being tested and evaluated.

Airbus A310.

February 14 was going to be my first overseas flight, from YYZ to Lisbon (LIS) on Airbus A310 C-GTSX, and I was looking forward to it. It was the first time I crossed the Atlantic Ocean as a pilot. Oceanic flying is complex yet fascinating, as hundreds of airplanes cross the ocean daily by using the North Atlantic Tracks (NAT) system.

The Atlantic Ocean Airspace is not controlled by a radar as it is over land. Instead, there are "imaginary" highways created daily by Gander and Shanwick control centers that the airplane's navigation systems will track crossing the ocean between Europe and North America. This oceanic airspace is between 28,500 and 41,000 feet. Airplanes are safely separated horizontally by each maintaining a constant Mach speed so as not to overtake one another while maintaining the same track route. The view from the cockpit is fascinating as airplanes are separated from one another by 1000 feet.

An oceanic flight starts in the crew room, where we'd review all documents and the flight plan. A well-detailed review of the Oceanic route, weather analysis enroute and of all alternate airports, the aircraft maintenance log, and NOTAMS are a few of the many things pilots verify before leaving the crew room and getting on the airplane.

Once inside the airplane, we set our flight bags by our seats, stored our personal suitcase, and headed to the cabin for the captain briefing to the cabin crew. On the A310, we had nine flight attendants, including one flight director who oversaw the cabin. The captain then gave a briefing to the crew, reviewing the flight information and the procedures in case of an emergency. This briefing was always a great time to meet the crew and have a chance to interact before the flight.

Then the fun began: the cockpit preparation and programming of the FMS. Two of us pilots operated that flight together. One of us was going to head outside and perform the aircraft's exterior walk-around. The walk-around was performed by the pilot who was going to be the pilot monitoring (PM) on this leg portion. Once that was complete, the PM got back on the airplane and performed the weight and balance calculations and ensured all the passengers, luggage, cargo, and fuel were balanced in the aircraft weight envelope.

Since I was the pilot flying (PF) on that leg, I took care of the preflight performance calculations. As I was programming the aircraft navigation systems, I was thinking to myself how amazing this was—I was about to fly an airplane across the ocean and have a chance to spend a day off in Lisbon. This was my first visit to Portugal, and I was so excited!

Once both of us completed our tasks, I performed the takeoff briefing and a review of the instrument departure procedure from YYZ. On that flight I was going to fly the aircraft, take off, and land in Lisbon while the PM communicated with Air Traffic Control, performed checklists, and completed all the paperwork.

Since the autopilot is mostly on during the entire flight, beside takeoff and landing, often people ask me what pilots do in the flight deck on a long flight Are we ever bored? The answer is that there is a lot that pilots do in the cruise portion of the flight, especially during an oceanic flight.

The first task of the PF is to make sure the airplane is navigating and maintaining a precise accuracy the whole flight. Even with the autopilot on, the PF must ensure the control of the aircraft is well maintained. The oceanic airspace is busy with many airplanes; therefore the navigation progress of the flight is extremely important. Also, during this time on the A310, the PM performs position reports via the high frequency (HF) radio, which can be a challenging task sometimes with many airplanes reporting positions at the same time. Today, with the Controller Direct Pilot Communication (CDPLC) system, positions reports are done automatically through the aircraft's communication system. The rest of the time, pilots perform fuel checks, weather analysis for the en route extended-range twin-engine operational performance standards (ETOPS) alternate airport, and if there is any weather up in the high altitudes, then operating the weather radar will be another task pilots are busy with.

The departure and cruise portion of the flight went smoothly. We were at 30W longitude over the mid-Atlantic Ocean, at 35,000 feet, late in the night, with the moon bright on the horizon and flying at speed of Mach 0.79 (approximately over 900 km/h). I glanced at my coffee cup and noticed there weren't any ripples in it; I was just amazed at how aviation and airplanes had evolved in just over a hundred years.

These magnificent machines can navigate so precisely and smoothly. I fell in love with my profession all over again. I could see myself doing this type of work for a very long time.

There is just something special about being up high in the air over the mid-Atlantic and seeing the sun rise on the horizon.

As we approached the Portuguese coast, we commenced our descent and joined the arrival route to Lisbon Airport. Breaking from the clouds as we turned final onto Runway 03, I was just amazed at the beauty of the city: the orange painted roofs, the Rio Tejo River that enters Lisbon from the Atlantic, and the massive bridges. To date, this view on an approach path to an airport is my favorite; it is just so scenic and beautiful.

The flight went well overall, and I was able to take lots of good notes to review for the return flight. We parked the airplane and made our way out from the terminal and towards the transport buses that would take us to the hotel.

The drive to the hotel was nice, and I was excited to do some sightseeing later that day. I could feel that a few hours of sleep would help, as now the jet lag was kicking in. Busy during the flight, I did not feel the tiredness of being up all night, but now it was hitting me while sitting on the bus.

Once we checked in the hotel, all the crew went to their assigned rooms for a well-deserved break. I made plans to meet the captain at 7:00 p.m. for dinner. After a few hours of sleep, I went out sightseeing in the city. The weather was nice and warm. Lisbon is a vibrant city, and I enjoyed walking around and taking pictures. Lisbon was my first layover overseas and is one of my favorite cities to layover in the world.

Up to this point in my career, I had flown different types of commercial flights: Northern flying, short flights on average of one to four hours, domestic flights, and flights between Canada, the United States, and the Caribbean. I must say that long-haul oceanic flying is my favorite.

Operating one takeoff and landing segment, landing in another country, and having a day off to explore is a great experience and a type of flying I really enjoy. But some prefer short domestic flights instead. The great thing is that the airline industry has many different options for pilots to choose from depending on what type of flying and lifestyle they would like to have. The important thing is that we get to fly, and the key is to enjoy every moment!

"We are getting paid to have dinner in Lisbon," I told the captain over dinner.

Does not get better than that!

COMMUNICATION FAILURE

On March 25, 2009, I was operating flight TSC322 from Toronto to London Gatwick. It was a special moment, not because I had a seventy-two-hour layover (lucky for me!), but my little brother, Nir, joined me on this pairing.

Overflying the Atlantic Ocean and the communications with Air Traffic Control were routine, with the standard position reports transmitted via HF to Shanwick Radio. We had a smooth four hours over the ocean until we reached the European coast, where communicating with Air Traffic Control was getting busy and challenging, as there were multiple six digits frequency changes with different control centers.

"Air Transat 322, new routing for you. Confirm ready to copy," the controller said.

"Go ahead, sir, ready to copy," I replied ready to write down the new clearance and then program the FMS with the new route.

Not long after we commenced our descent through approximately 10,000 feet, we were now transferred to London Arrival Air Traffic Control. I was working the radios while the captain was the PF.

"London Control, good morning. Air Transat 322 level 100, on descent level 80," I informed the controller.

Usually the controller responds right away, but surprisingly this time, there was no response. I tried again, but still no reply.

Interestingly, sometimes when there is a shift change between controllers, there can be a couple of seconds of silence through the transition, but in this case it was unusual for such busy airspace. I checked the frequency; it was the correct one. I switched back to the previous frequency to confirm there was no error and now even the previous controller was not responding.

"I'll try the other radio," I told the captain as he was monitoring the autopilot during the descent to flight level 8000 feet.

I tried contacting Air Traffic Control again but still had no success with either radios or even the emergency radio frequency. Could this be my first communications failure? This wasn't the airspace a pilot or controller would want to be in with such a failure—it's one of the busiest airspaces in the world!

The first thing I had to do in this situation was relax. The top priority is always for one pilot to fly the airplane while the other troubleshoots the problem. In this situation, I was the troubleshooter. I selected the comm failure code on the airplane transponder, which would send a message to the controller that we were experiencing technical problems with our radios and unable to communicate.

After consulting the Quick Reference Handbook (QRH), the checklist recommended resetting any control wheel transmission switch. Done! Then I glanced at the radio panel and looked at every switch to make sure everything was pressed or selected accordingly. I reset every single switch on the audio control panel (ACP) to see if anything was stuck in there, then did that on both panels.

"London Control, radio check for Air Transat 322," I called, hoping everything I did had resolved the issue.

"Air Transat 322, loud and clear. How about me?" the controller came up on the radio.

Relief!

"Five-by-five, sir, we had a glitch with the comms. All normal now," I replied.

"Good job, Gerry!" the captain said happily. We did not have to end up doing a long, complicated comm failure procedure into one of the busiest airports in the world.

I had a nice seventy-two-hour layover with my brother in London. Always fun having family join you at work!

Nir and I in Toronto, prior to the departure to London, UK October 2010

THE AIRBUS A330

When working for a major airline, the chance that the pilots will be unionized is highly likely. This has its advantages and disadvantages. I am not going to list all of them, as this is only my opinion and everyone has their own, but what is important to mention is that when unionized, every pilot receives a seniority number, which enables them to "bid" for a position or an opening. Depending on the placement of a pilot's seniority number, they will be able to obtain their bid choice. Pilots bid for monthly schedules, vacation periods, promotions, pilot bases, and charter contracts, just to name a few. Even if layoffs occur, this seniority number will determine if the pilot will be able to keep their current position or get a layoff notice.

In August 2010, almost three years after getting hired by Air Transat, I had the opportunity to bid for the position of FO on the Airbus A330. The A330 is a wide-body, state-of-the-art, long-range aircraft; it has a 3700-kilometer greater range than the A310 and has a digital fly-by-wire controls system.

The fly-by-wire system operates the flight controls of the aircraft by interpreting the pilot's inputs that he or she makes on the sidestick.

The A330 I've flown have a 350 to 375 passenger configuration, which also includes a first-class section.

As a pilot, I've always wanted to learn, advance in my career, and fly modern and advanced aircraft; hence, this was a great opportunity for me. The beauty was that the airline paid for the whole training program, which is extremely expensive in the case of the A330 ($60,000 per pilot). Although switching aircraft type, my seniority number had me held in a junior position on the aircraft when it came to monthly schedules and vacation choices, but the opportunity outweighed the lifestyle change. Some will prefer a better schedule than an aircraft type.

The A330 served destinations that I was looking forward to flying to, such as Athens and Rome, where the A310 would not serve due to its range. Also, the A330 has a side stick instead of a conventional control column—a technology I was looking forward to learning about. The A330 has an incredibly quiet cockpit compared to many other jets, making the work environment amazingly comfortable for pilots. I should also mention that the A330 is a beauty of an aircraft!

Departure from Montreal (YUL) Airbus A330 July 2018

I was awarded the position of FO and started simulator training in early September 2010. As I did in the past, I prepared a study list of the material I would need to review before the start of training. I reviewed the SOP first, then all flows, memory items, and checklists, and completed all online aircraft systems courses. Since we were two

FOs paired together, the captain's flows and memory items had to also be memorized and performed in the simulator and the final flight test.

The simulator training sessions began on September 6, and the final simulator flight test was a month later, on October 5. On that date, I officially had the EA33 type rating on my license—the fifth type of aircraft certified on my license and the biggest airplane I had ever flown to date in my career. The first line indoctrination flight was on October 7, from YUL to CDG Paris (CDG), flight TS410, on aircraft Airbus A330-300, registration C-GKTS, which is the longer version A330.

Despite the airplane being bigger and heavier than the A310 by 80 tons, hand-flying the airplane was simple. Contrary to what some may think, the bigger the airplane, the simpler it is to fly. There are so many systems assisting the pilot, which makes handling the aircraft a lot simpler and more straightforward.

On a turboprop airplane like a Metroliner or King Air, there is a lot more force required on the control wheel compared to the sidestick of the A330. On the other hand, the bigger the airplane, the more complex the systems. The pilot's job becomes more of a managerial task than just flying. Also, since the airplane is bigger, it carries a lot more energy and therefore momentum, which requires better planning from the pilot, for example, during descent and approach due to its inertia.

It is therefore especially important to be well stabilized on final approach to the runway by the 1000-feet above-ground mark in the landing configuration. Being perfectly lined up with the runway and touching down exactly in the landing zone is vital, as due to its size there is not much room for error.

I enjoyed flying the aircraft and the working environment of the cockpit, which was like no other airplane. The cockpit is roomy, and even when standing up, there is lots of room to move around without hitting your head on any overhead switches.

Airbus A330, Dominican Republic November 2010

The magical view from the office.

Approximately five months after my initial training on the A330, I was scheduled for my first recurrent training in the simulator. Airline pilots return in the sim every six months to train and to get evaluated. Since this was my first recurrent on the airplane and with only 250 hours flown since initial training, I started reviewing and preparing for this simulator session a couple of months in advance.

Recurrent training comprises one training session of four hours, followed by a four-hour flight test the next day, which includes several abnormal situations, takeoffs with engine failures, landing on one engine, and low visibility automatic landings.

For this recurrent training, I also applied for a captain evaluation. I was ready for this evaluation process, and during the last few months I had received positive feedback from the captains I had flown with, who suggested I should be asking for the evaluation from the chief pilot.

The captain evaluation process is straightforward. In this simulator flight test, I was going to be evaluated by the check pilot to see if I had the skills, knowledge, leadership, and overall performance to eventually be trained as a captain.

I had to do well in this training and the flight test, as a negative evaluation would prevent me from re-applying until another eighteen months had passed. Also, since this was my first recurrent on the airplane, the pressure was on to do well.

My application was approved by the chief pilot, and my captain evaluation simulator session took place on March 30, 2011. It was successful. This meant I was able to bid for the next open captain positions.

There is no secret formula for a good sim training and flight test. A pilot needs to review all study material in advance and be well prepared for simulator and line training—it's part of our profession. The best way to face these challenges first is by a positive attitude, a learning and progressing mindset. Also, time management is important during preparation, but you should also try to be relaxed no matter how difficult the evaluations can be. When one is calm, better decisions will be made. I used this mindset throughout my career and put it to the test on my captain upgrade training on the Airbus A310.

CAPTAIN UPGRADE TRAINING
ON A WIDE-BODY JET

I received a call from the chief pilot letting me know that my upgrade captain training on the Airbus A310 would commence in a month. With the company's expansion and some retirements, the upgrade positions got to my seniority number. I was so happy with this amazing news, knowing I now had a shot at becoming a captain on a wide-body jet for a major airline.

At that time I was flying the A330, but since I was still current on the A310, the upgrade training consisted of four training simulator sessions and then the fifth session, the final flight test. Once that stage was complete, I would need approximately 100 flight hours of line training with an instructor acting as the FO and a final line check before getting the "keys to the big truck."

I knew this would probably be the biggest challenge of my career to date. I was going back from the A330 to the A310. Although I already flew the airplane, I still had lots of reviewing to do as both airplanes are quite different as far as the design philosophy, flight characteristics, and overall greater workload from the pilots. I had a great deal of preparation and studying ahead of me and knew that in the next couple of months, I would be spending all my time in the books.

I made a list of the manuals and documents I would need to review before simulator training. I started reading the SOPs and completing all the online training. I met up with my simulator partner, and we reviewed all the checklist, flows, and drills together. Studying with your sim partner is a great way to learn, as you can correct each other and it's more fun than studying alone.

Upgrade simulator training was demanding since many different scenarios and malfunctions are being reviewed in very busy simulator sessions. I had four busy simulator training sessions between May 22–25, and my final simulator flight test was completed on May 26, 2011.

The next phase of the program was line training. This stage would be the most challenging for many reasons. Many unexpected situations may happen during these flights since these are on live revenue flights and not scripted, whereas the simulator training sessions were. Therefore, as situations arise during these 100 hours of line training, it will be up to me to demonstrate leadership, good crew resource management (CRM), knowledge, and decision-making while facing these situations. It was also going to be important to demonstrate good knowledge of the company's procedures and regulations because as a captain I would be ultimately responsible for safe operations.

The first flight sitting in the captain's seat and leading the show was on June 3, on aircraft C-FDAT, from YYZ to (SNU) Cuba. During these flights, the instructors looked for a positive progression and constant learning and improvement from one flight to the other. For example, taxiing the airplane might not be perfect on the first flight or the landing, but during the next one and the one after, improvement should be demonstrated. Towards the end of the line training, the captain trainee should demonstrate mastering their new position and be ready for the line check.

It was going to be important for me, as a captain trainee, to demonstrate departing on time and maintaining on-time performance. If I was unable to demonstrate how to prevent or manage delays caused by a variety of factors as they came up, I would not obtain good grades. I showed up to work earlier than needed so that I had plenty of time to go over all the flight paperwork. I also had to be one step ahead during the cockpit preparation, anticipate things, and be able to delegate tasks. There are many people involved in a departure of an airliner; therefore, delegating and using good crew resources is also key.

There are many documents and manuals to review before a flight, such as the aircraft maintenance log and, in some cases, what is called minimum equipment list (MEL) items procedures. Some aircraft systems or components can be deactivated or not functioning before an aircraft departs on a flight, so pilots need to review and perform the applicable procedures before the flight. Other documents pilots verify include en route weather reports, the flight plan route, and fuel planning, Extended Oceanic Operations alternate airports weather conditions and availability of emergency services, the verification of GPS navigation coverage, and much more.

I was enjoying line training very much and was learning a lot from the experienced instructor pilots I was flying with. Each one of them shared their knowledge, helpful tips, and their own experiences. I took many notes during those flights and reviewed them often, as there was a lot to remember.

One memorable flight during my captain training was on June 17, when I operated a flight from YYZ to Heathrow (LHR). As I was walking in the terminal behind the cabin crew, I thought to myself that twenty-six years ago, I was here at this same terminal. I was only ten years old then, pushing a baggage cart with my two-year-old brother on it, entertaining him while we were waiting countless hours for our connecting flight; we were immigrating to Canada.

And there I was, after all these years, parking an Airbus A310 airplane at the gate while doing my captain training. Who could have imagined I would be at that same terminal so many years later? It is always interesting how life brings us back to places we have been before.

I was grateful for my parents and my family; I would not have made it to this special moment if not for their love, encouragement, and sacrifices.

The last training flight as a captain was completed on July 23, 2011. I had accumulated a total of ninety-five hours. I had three days to review all my notes and material again; my captain line check was scheduled on July 26, three days later.

★ ★ ★

The big day had arrived! Suitcase and flight bag all packed, I left my condo in downtown Toronto. As I was on my way to the parking lot, I knew this captain line check on a wide-body jet for a major airline would be one of the most important flights of my career.

I showed up early for the flight, before my check pilot arrived. I looked over the flight plan, the oceanic filed route, the planned fuel for the flight, the weather for all the alternate oceanic Extended Twin Engine Ops (ETOPS) airports, the technical status of the airplane, and the NOTAMS and prepared my notes for the briefing I would give to the flight attendants once at the airplane.

Once the check pilot showed up in the crew room, all the paperwork was reviewed and highlighted. My final stage of the upgrade training was a flight from YYZ to Amsterdam Schiphol (AMS) airport. I had flown with the check pilot previously on my first captain line training flight back in June.

On the YYZ–AMS segment, I was the PF, which allowed the check pilot to evaluate many points in the line check form, including the takeoff, the approach, and then the landing in Amsterdam. I was going to be evaluated and graded on thirty tasks, so everything I did had to be done perfectly well.

I called Dispatch for a pre-flight briefing, and off we were, heading to the airplane that was parked at gate C32 in Terminal 3. Once in the flight deck with flight bags in place, I briefed the cabin crew. This was my chance to meet the flight attendants and review and share important points about the flight. The check pilot then headed outside to perform the aircraft walk-around while I programmed and prepared the cockpit for departure. Weight and balance calculations were being finalized as the FD walked into the cockpit: "We are ready to start boarding, Captain."

As passengers were boarding, I completed the takeoff briefing and we reviewed the departure procedure. Once all the paperwork was signed and logbooks on board, I gave the thumbs up to close the main cabin door. Push back and short taxi to Runway 23 was all performed well. We were the number five aircraft in line, one after another on the taxiway, waiting for our takeoff clearance. The excitement began to build up; we were going to be airborne in a few minutes. So far so good!

Smooth rotation, and off we were, airborne and then getting vectors from Departure Control to join the standard instrument departure (SID) towards the east. I focused on making sure I was one step ahead, anticipating what was coming up in the flight. Before a flight, everything is already planned, but pilots make decisions constantly as things progress during different phases of the flight; hence, I made sure I was always ahead of the game.

Cruise checks and fuel and navigation checks were all completed, and all systems were working well. A couple of hours later, we picked up our oceanic clearance to join the NAT oceanic tracks—the Atlantic Ocean crossing track that we would follow all along the North Atlantic until the European coast.

Once we had the chance to each have our meals, we reviewed the engine drift down and emergency descent memory drills. These drills were reviewed countless times in training and in my condo, staring at my cockpit posters as I was studying.

At thirty degrees longitude over the Atlantic Ocean, I took the time to review all the approach charts for Amsterdam Schiphol Airport. I reviewed the airport arrival procedures and comm failure section and familiarized myself with the type of approach we would conduct, the airport runway diagram, and taxi procedures before the descent despite the fact I flew to that airport many times before.

Approach briefing completed, about an hour later we received descent clearance. We were authorized the arrival STAR and to expect the ILS approach to Runway 18R as we previously briefed.

"Air Transat 351, would you like to transition to Runway 18C?" the tower controller asked us over the radio as we were turning final to Runway 18R. What the controller wanted to know was if we wanted to switch our approach to the center runway.

"You want it?" the check pilot asked me.

This was the situation: I was established and stabilized on the final approach to Runway 18R in the landing configuration. Once on the ground, the taxi time to the terminal would be at least twenty minutes or more, which would be an extra amount of fuel consumption. On the other hand, breaking off from the approach from Runway 18R to the center runway would have involved disconnecting the autopilot, hand-flying the airplane to the other runway, and getting out of a perfectly stabilized approach. Landing on the center runway would be more economical as far as fuel was concerned, but if for whatever reason I would get destabilized, I would have to pull up from the approach and go around.

"No, unable. We'll stay on the approach," I replied.

It was not the most economical decision, but the safest one considering my comfort level. I was not going to risk changing the approach and getting destabilized. Rather safe than sorry!

After landing, I cleared the active runway and called for the shutting down of engine number two to save on fuel as we were taxiing now single engine to the parking apron. The taxiing to the parking position took forever, and I was picturing in my mind the check pilot probably laughing to himself.

We had a twenty-four-hour layover in Amsterdam. On the way back to Toronto, I was evaluated on my duties as the pilot not flying (PNF) while the check pilot did the takeoff in Amsterdam and the landing in Toronto.

After landing in Toronto and as we slowed to taxi speed, I took control of the aircraft from the check pilot and taxied the airplane to the passenger Terminal 3. The test was almost done!

"No pressure, but all you got left is the next five minutes and you're a captain, Gerry," the check pilot said.

"I can't wait to celebrate," I replied with a smile on my face.

I lined up the airplane with the ground marshaller and was now taxiing the airplane by scanning ahead, confirming we were all cleared from obstacles. As we were approaching the parking position,

I transitioned, looking at the Advanced Visual Docking Guidance System (A-VDGS), which was helping me park the airplane in the exact designated spot.

With the parking brake on and auxiliary power unit (APU) checked "on" I put both engines fuel switches to the cut-off position. As the engines spooled down, I turned off the seat belts sign and exterior beacon. "Parking checklist, please!" I called out.

"Congrats, Captain!" With a smile on his face, the check pilot extended his hand to shake mine. He removed his captain epaulettes from his shirt and replaced my FO epaulettes. It was a special moment.

There I was, thirty-six years old and a captain on a big jet for Air Transat. No words could describe how I felt. It was a huge accomplishment and one of the highlights of my career. Just under four years earlier I had been hired by the airline, and now I was a captain! It is amazing what we can achieve when we want something.

Flying as a captain has its responsibilities, but it is also very gratifying, fulfilling, and most of all, enjoyable. To be the leader of a team has always been something I enjoy doing. It is a great accomplishment for an airline pilot, and a position I enjoy to this day.

Airbus A310, Toronto, July 2011.

Aviation has its ups and downs. Unfortunately, close to a year and a half after getting promoted to a captain position, I was downgraded back to an FO, as were many of my colleagues in the same situation as me.

With the posted down-bid, my seniority number was not able to secure me a captain position, and in November of 2012 I received a call from Flight Ops that I was scheduled to report to the A310 simulator to get requalified on the right seat as an FO.

It was the only time I found myself in the flight simulator not wanting to be there. It was hard to accept that everything I had worked for to become a captain, and earning and maintaining that position with good performance, was now taken away from me.

When a doctor becomes a surgeon, they do not suddenly become an assistant in an operating room one day and have all responsibilities and a leadership role they once held taken away from them. In many professions, once a person has achieved a specific level or position, they do not usually get demoted, but in aviation it does happen. It was hard to accept, but I had no other choice. At least I was still employed and flying. Could have been worse.

Six months later, after flying 218 flight hours as an FO, I was informed that I would be able to return to my previous permanent captain position. One training flight and a line check later, and I was back in the left seat. It felt great!

Like myself, many of my colleagues returned to flying as captains, but some unfortunately had to stay FOs a little longer, even for almost a whole year. It was good to see everyone eventually regain their captain position, and to see the industry return on a positive trend.

Airbus A330, Marseille, July 2018.

Throughout my career similar events had happened, where I found myself holding a good position until a global or financial situation affected the industry and I found myself downgraded. It is something myself and many other airline pilots have faced; some more than others in their aviation career.

BIRDS DO STRIKE

I was operating a flight from Edmonton Airport (YEG) to Puerto Vallarta (PVR) and back to Edmonton on the A310 in the summer of 2012. The flight to PVR was straightforward, besides of course the demanding mountainous arc procedure STAR approach that pilots need to perform into PVR, which will eventually position the aircraft on the final approach to Runway 22.

We were at the gate just a little over an hour before commencing the push back and taxi to Runway 22. It was a 1:00 a.m. departure for a night flight back to Edmonton.

The control tower cleared us for takeoff as we approached the departure runway, and once I lined up the aircraft, I gave control to the FO, who was the PF on that leg.

"Runway 22, heading 222," Pierre called out, confirming we were on the correct runway and that our instruments confirmed the runway heading. He then triggered the autothrust buttons located under the thrust levers, which then automatically positioned the thrust levers to the pre-determined takeoff power setting.

"Thrust set," I called out, and then Pierre removed his left hands from the thrust levers. I then put my right hand on the thrust levers, in case I had to perform a rejected takeoff procedure.

The takeoff roll was smooth; Pierre kept the airplane straight on the runway, as he was waiting to gain speed so he would be able to safely pull back on the control wheel to take off. That is the VR (rotation speed), which on that day was 150 knots (277 km/h).

There is also one more speed to bear in mind: decision speed (V1), which was 148 knots on that takeoff. As per Airbus, V1 is the maximum speed at which a rejected takeoff can be initiated in the event of an emergency. V1 is also the minimum speed at which a pilot can continue the takeoff following an engine failure. All these speeds are given by a performance program that calculates all the takeoff speeds depending on weight, weather conditions, and many other factors. Pilots will insert these speeds in the FMS.

As we approached decision speed, we both saw the countless large birds crossing the runway right in front of the windshield. At the same time, we heard a loud metallic "*bang*"; it felt as if some of the birds had hit the nose wheel. I quickly glanced at the engine's main instruments; everything seemed to work well.

"Continue," I called out so that Pierre remained at the controls and continued the takeoff roll.

At such a high speed, so close to V1, with no engine failure, it was time to get airborne and deal with the problem in the air, otherwise we risked aborting the takeoff and ending up off the runway. As speed approaches V1, the successful completion of a rejected takeoff becomes increasingly more difficult, as explained by Airbus.

Pierre made the rotation at VR speed, and the mighty A310 got airborne with no issues. We knew that a bird hit part of the airplane, but where was unknown to us at that moment.

I analyzed all aircraft systems as Pierre was flying; everything seemed to be working well, with no issues with any system or the engines. I advised the tower of the bird strike, and after inspecting the runway, they could not find any bird remains.

The rest of the flight was uneventful, and a textbook approach and landing was made by Pierre.

Sometimes pilots have time to make decisions and other times a fraction of a second. It's the nature of the job and situations that pilots are often faced with. It was a good reminder that staying focused throughout a flight, especially during critical phases, is very important where decisions will have to be made in a split second.

EXAMPLE OF CREW RESOURCE MANAGEMENT (CRM)

The roots of crew resource management (CRM) go back to a workshop named "Resource Management on the Flight Deck," sponsored by the National Aeronautics and Space Administration in 1979.

The research was to understand the causes of air transport accidents. It was identified that human error of most air accidents were failures of interpersonal communications, decision making, and leadership. At this meeting, the title cockpit resource management (CRM) was applied to the process of training flight crews to reduce "pilot error" by making better use of the human resources and communication on the flight deck.

The airlines have invested a lot in CRM training for pilots, flight attendants, and mechanics. One of the things I learned in my upgrade captain CRM training is to use all the resources available. That means when in a normal situation or an emergency, you make the decisions with as much information that is available at that time. Everyone in the team or crew is an asset to the captain, whether an FO, a flight attendant, a fueler, or dispatcher.

The primary goal of CRM is having good situational awareness, leadership, assertiveness, decision making, being open minded and to listen, flexibility, adaptability, and mostly communication. The captain sets the culture and environment where everyone in the crew feels valuable and comfortable to speak up and to work as a team. It's not about who is right but what is right!

We were en route from Birmingham, UK, to Toronto on the Airbus A310 aircraft C-GTSY in September 2012. Due to the runway and weather conditions in Birmingham, there was a high probability we would have to make a tech stop en route, due to weight and balance restrictions on departure.

As we approached the Canadian coast and after consulting with our dispatcher, the decision was made to make a tech stop in Gander,

Newfoundland. On the A310, a procedure existed that the fuel in the outer tanks would need to be consumed for forty-five minutes, an hour and a half before arrival, when the temperature at the destination is between -5°C and +5°C. Not performing this procedure would likely result in frost accumulated over the top outer part of the wing upon arrival, which would result in a trip to the de-ice facility prior to departure.

The tech stop was quick. Once at the gate, we received our new flight plans and waited for the fuel truck to arrive. My FO was getting ready to leave the flight deck and head outside to perform the exterior walk-around. It was a beautiful sunny and +20°C that afternoon in Gander.

At that same moment, Amanda, one of our flight attendants, walked in the flight deck.

"Hi, guys, quick question. Have you been outside yet?" Amanda asked.

"No, actually, I was just heading outside for the aircraft walk-around," replied Jeff.

"Ah, ok, because I think the wings will need to be de-iced!"

Amanda was right. Despite it being 20°C and warm outside, with our short thirty-minute turnaround the combination of cold fuel in the outer tank and the warm upper wing surface created frost on the outer top part of the wing, which needed to be removed before departure.

Since the de-ice trucks were not available at that time, we got a hand from the airport's fire truck, which had to spray warm water on the top of the wing to melt the accumulated frost.

The moral of the story is not to review the A310 fuel system, but rather mention that Amanda saw something that did not seem right and brought the question up to the pilots. We took that valuable information and did something about it which was to inspect the wings.

During the preflight crew briefing, I always bring up the point that there is no such thing as a stupid question. If there is a concern, don't be afraid to bring up a comment or any question that comes to mind.

When in doubt, ask, and if you are in the authority position listen, consider and act accordingly. Use all information available and each person in your team. That is what CRM is all about! A captain that does not have that mindset will end up making decisions alone, which is the worst thing a pilot can do, unless you are flying a single-pilot airplane.

EVIDENCE-BASED TRAINING (EBT)

In 2012, I received a phone call from one of the company's captains who was given the task of assembling a team that would build a new training program for the pilots called Evidence-Based Training (EBT). This training philosophy is different from what most airlines had been using for many years. Instead of giving pilots a simulator training session followed by a PPC test every six months, pilots would have the opportunity to practice real events that previously occurred on the specific type of airplane for the airline or any other airlines.

The advantages are the elimination of the stressful flight test on pilots, and instead of the repetitive style of training, pilots would have a variety of training exercises involving more aircraft maneuvers and a review of real-time industry flight events.

I see great advantages in this training philosophy where pilots will gain valuable knowledge from real events, a program which focuses on pilot development and assessment of key pilot competencies to better prepare the pilot to deal with various situations.

I was happy to be selected and to join the team on this new project. I had the opportunity to learn about the EBT program while spending time with Air France's flight crews during their simulator sessions in France.

CHAPTER 8

✈

ASSISTANT CHIEF PILOT (SUPERVISOR)

When working for a major airline, there are many opportunities available for pilots to advance and gain more skills or experience. Pilots can choose to become an instructor in the simulator or give ground courses, become a check pilot, give line checks or simulator tests, work in the Flight Safety Department, and much more.

In 2013, Air Transat was operating the A330 and A310 aircrafts but was planning to add another type of airplane to its fleet: the Boeing B737 800 Next Generation (NG).

The Boeing 737NG is a narrow-body and stretch version of the 737-700 model. The model was launched in 1993 as the third-generation derivative of the Boeing 737, which is an upgrade of the 737 Classic series.

This new type of airplane in the fleet required a new team in the Flight Operations Department, which had to consist of a chief pilot to oversee all operations of that airplane, and assistants called supervisors to help him with his tasks.

I decided to apply for the supervisor position, although I knew there were many highly skilled pilots applying for this position as it rarely became available. I'd always wanted to join the training department and was confident I had the right background to be an asset to the Flight Ops team.

A supervisor is also a check pilot type-rated examiner (TRE), which would enable me to instruct and test pilots in the simulator and the airplane. I would be responsible for assisting in the supervision of the daily flight operations, building training and test scripts, and preparing and giving pilot recurrent courses and instructor meetings. I would be part of the pilot interview team and be on call for any situations where the flight crew or any other department would require support.

Besides those tasks mentioned, I would also be able to fly regular revenue flights; though this was a challenging position, it had great rewards. It would also be a great opportunity for me to learn a new airplane, and since I had never flown a Boeing aircraft before, I was looking forward to the opportunity.

I had to go through an interview for this position, which was given by the new chief pilot, who was also part of my initial interview panel with the airline back in 2007. He was joined by a Human Resources representative.

The interview was mostly an opportunity for the chief pilot to get to know me a little more, understand the reason I was applying for the position, and see if I had the personality and knowledge to be selected to this position.

The interview was a success, and I was officially promoted to the supervisor position in December 2013. Holding the position of supervisor was the highlight of my career. It was a position that came with great responsibilities, which required many operational decisions that had a direct impact on the airline's operations.

To become a supervisor, I had to first be type rated on the new airplane, which required a month and a half of training. I also had to pass all the tests and requirements to become a check pilot, learn the managerial duties in the Flight Operations Department, and familiarize myself with many of the aviation regulations used to run the department and the pilot training requirements. By learning all these tasks, I had the opportunity to see how the chains and bolts of an airline worked—something line pilots don't get the chance to see.

For a supervisor, the job never ended once the parking brake was set on arrival at the gate. My cell phone was always on and ready to take calls. The schedule was busy and demanding, requiring great time management. Many deadlines had to be met, such as preparing courses and documents on time.

We would have what is called "weekend duty," where one supervisor is responsible to answer phone calls from various departments depending on the situation. For example, we'd get questions from Crew Scheduling regarding a pilot training flight, from an instructor in the simulator having a delay or an issue, from a pilot in Europe about a route filed on their flight plan, and so on. There was even a time I received a call transferred to me by a Flight Dispatcher directly from a pilot via SATCOM (satellite communications) who was over the Atlantic and had a technical question requiring assistance. There are many situations requiring input or support from a supervisor.

Overall, despite its responsibilities and no room for error, the position was very exciting, and I enjoyed all the challenges and rewards it brought. We just never stop learning as pilots, and even though I'd been in the industry for many years already, I learned every day as a supervisor.

A pilot masters a skill by growing and learning. The best way to learn is by acquiring new projects and challenges through your career, such as instructing, examining, or upper management flying positions. With these positions come great perks as well.

Turning final on to Runway 24R in YUL, B737-800 NG.

TWICE IN ALASKA

The first of the company's B737 was leased from an airline from France, and the plan was to ferry four sister-ships aircraft from Malaysia.

I had a chance to ferry two of the four airplanes from Malaysia and Alaska. The first ferry flight I flew was for aircraft registration C-GTQF, seven hours flight time from Anchorage, Alaska to Rome, New York (RME) airport, on June 29, 2014. The second ferry flight was for airplane registration C-GTQG ferried from Subang, Malaysia (SZB), at the end of August. I had always wanted to visit Alaska, and I finally got to go twice in one summer, both unbelievable experiences.

Before leaving Canada to Malaysia for one of the ferry flights, I called Visa to inform them that I would be going to a few countries in the following week so they would not think someone stole my credit card. Once on the phone with the agent, I informed her that I would be leaving Canada to Paris, then on to Malaysia, to Nagoya, Japan, then Anchorage, Alaska, before a final stop at Trois-Rivières, Quebec.

"How long will you be away for, sir? A couple of weeks?" she asked.

"No, ma'am, less than a week," I replied.

"Oh, wow, what line of work do you do, 007?" She laughed and so did I.

Who said phone agents don't have a sense of humor?

The mission started with my FO and I meeting at the Air France premium lounge, where we had a chance to talk about our journey and, of course, eat some delicious food before our first-class deadhead to Paris on the queen of the skies, the B747. The departure was early at 5:30 p.m., which got us to Paris (CDG) airport at midnight.

Once arrived in CDG, within an hour we were at the Sheraton Hotel, at the check-in counter right at the airport terminal. The next day, our flight with Malaysia Airlines to Malaysia was at 7:00 p.m., which allowed us to get some good rest at the hotel.

The flight was comfortable but very long. We finally arrived at the hotel in the late afternoon. I texted our lead mechanic, who was overseeing all the ferry flights, and informed him that we had arrived. That was the last ferry flight; therefore, the fourth B737 the company was bringing to Canada. The good thing about ferry flights was we always had a mechanic on board.

Kuala Lumpur is a very nice and modern city. We checked in at the hotel and headed to our respective rooms on the hotel's high floors. I have stayed in many nice hotels in my career and travels, but the room I stayed in was one of the biggest and most luxurious rooms I've ever stayed in. It had an office, a huge bathroom, and a living room as well. I wondered if they had mistaken me for another guest.

Jet lag didn't help this time, and after a few hours of sleep I woke up early to start looking at the flight documents, then called Dispatch to get a flight briefing for our first leg of the ferry flight to Nagoya, Japan. I then reviewed the airport diagram, taxi, and departure procedures, went over the flight plan, and familiarized myself with all the alternate airports we had en route in case of any problems.

The flight plan was straightforward: seven hours long, a little weather en route, but nothing major.

"Gerry, the airplane is ready," the mechanic texted me.

"Check, we're leaving the hotel then," I replied. I waited for that text before we left the hotel so we didn't waste our duty time at the airport in case of delays and the airplane was not released from maintenance.

We arrived at the airport, went through security and immigration, and had a truck drive us to the cargo parking where the airplane was supposed to be. As we approached the apron, there was no B737 outside. The baby Boeing was still inside the hangar with two huge B777 blocking it.

We got into the flight deck and started our tasks as much as we could while maintenance was finishing the final paperwork. Not long after, the airplane was towed outside and we were able to do a thorough walk-around.

We were all set up, with all doors closed. We had our lead mechanic in the jumpseat with us and the second mechanic in the cabin. I was to perform the takeoff and be the PF to Japan in case we had any malfunctions on departure.

We had good engine starts, with just a small issue with one of the generators that took its time to come online. It took a minute for it to get up to speed, and off we were, taxiing for takeoff en route to Japan.

During the cruise portion, we had some interesting weather build-ups to work with and to deviate around. These were different weather storms, and the formations of altocumulus/cumulonimbus clouds had vastly different shapes from the ones we were used to seeing in North America. The cloud formations were extremely high in altitude compared to the ones in North America. But they were easier to deviate around, as they were more locally organized and not formed in long, wide walls as we would often see in the flights towards the Caribbean from Canada. Those build-ups were impressive, though. We were at 40,000 feet, and it seemed like the top of these clouds were at 60,000 feet or higher.

During the flight, we were often busy communicating with ATC and negotiating weather deviation clearances so we could avoid all that weather. Eventually, we cleared all the weather and started our approach from the south to Chubu Centrair International Airport. The international airport is on an artificial island in Ise Bay, Tokoname City, thirty-five kilometers south of Nagoya in central Japan. The arrival at the airport was straightforward until we heard a loud alarm sounding in the cockpit during the last half mile of the approach to land. That got our attention since it is not usually a place you would want to have any malfunction with the airplane when you are just about to land.

It was the smoke detector, which was known to activate due to humidity that was entering the cabin during the descent—a system glitch. I focused on the approach and flying the airplane since we were about to touch down. Once on the ground, the mechanic we had on board was able to cancel the alarm.

We parked the airplane in a remote designated area, shut down the engines, secured the airplane, and proceeded to clear customs and immigration. Not long after, the four of us were in a taxi heading to the hotel, which was approximately an hour's drive. The hotel we had reservations at was nothing compared to the one in Malaysia. We were all staying on the same floor, and as soon as we walked into our designated rooms, we all came out at the same time. The four of us looked at each other and said, "There's no way we can stay in this place." The rooms were so tiny.

As I opened a small little window in the room, a blast of dust flew in my face; we were facing a construction site behind the hotel.

I called the Crew Scheduling Department and told them that we would have to stay in another hotel and cancel the one we were at. I then went online and used the company credit card to book a more adequate hotel right at the airport so we wouldn't have to drive long the next day.

It was already dinner time when we arrived at the airport hotel; everyone was in the mood for beef for dinner, but not me. Sushi is my favorite food, and there was no way I was not going to be feasting on that while in Japan.

The front desk recommended I stay in the airport, which had a sushi restaurant still open at that time. I quickly changed and headed to grab some sushi. I walked into the restaurant and took a seat at the bar, which I found interesting since it had a faucet at every station. I was starving by that time and was ready to order everything on the menu, which was all in Japanese. That was no issue, as all I had to do was point to the pictures of what I wanted in the menu.

I have sushi almost all over the world and at the fanciest restaurants, but nothing could have compared to the sushi in Japan. The rice was just so soft, and the salmon the freshest I ever had. I had a fabulous dinner, and I admit I ordered so much food, probably enough for the whole crew if they were with me.

I woke up the next morning ready to look at all the flight paperwork and documents, then called Dispatch for a briefing. The good thing about this leg was that the airplane was already fueled and no maintenance work was needed, besides a walk-around and maintenance standard pre-flight inspection that our mechanics would have taken care of once arriving at the airport.

The departure from Nagoya went without a glitch, and off we were, heading to Alaska. Since the whole flight would keep us over the ocean, we made sure to get updated weather reports for our en route alternates. Fuel was not an issue on this leg since we left with full tanks, but knowing where to go in case of an emergency was very important.

After seven hours and fifteen minutes, it was time to start the descent to Ted Stevens Anchorage International Airport (ANC). The descent to Anchorage was beautiful, as the sun was setting, the light reflecting on the stunning mountain range despite the fact it was 9:00 p.m. and still light out. As we flew abeam Lake Clark National Park from the south, we were cleared by Arrival Control to join the final approach to Runway 07L.

En route from Nagoya with Japan's iconic Mount Fuji profile in sight, August 2014.

By the time we parked and exited the airplane, it was close to midnight. The great thing was that the next day we'd be free to go sightseeing, and I could not wait for that.

On descent and on arrival to Ted Stevens Anchorage International Airport in Alaska, with a beautiful view from the office.

The following day, I woke up early and headed out for a long walk and sightseeing. The first thing I noticed about Alaska was how fresh the air was, and I was taking in the beauty of that amazing place. Also, every person you spoke to was so friendly. It felt like you were in a very relaxed and easy-going city. After a few hours of walking, I headed back to the hotel to rest and then meet up with the rest of the crew for dinner.

The next day, we departed Anchorage for Trois-Rivières, Quebec. The flight was just under seven hours long, and we had a chance to overfly Yukon and the Northwest Territories. Once landed, we had customs agents ready to clear our entry, and then we met up with the maintenance team, who made the conversion of the aircraft to our airline's standards.

This ferry flight was such a great and fun experience. The opportunity to see so many beautiful places, fly over beautiful sights, and complete an important mission for the airline was second to none. With those ferry flights I was introduced to a new operation that business jet pilots are usually faced with. The logistics and operation of ferry flying are quite different than airline operations. In ferry operations, more planning responsibilities fall on the pilots versus in the airlines, where more assistance is available from Dispatch and other departments.

TWO AIRPLANES AT THE SAME ALTITUDE

January 15, 2015, I was giving a line check to another colleague and a company check pilot on the B737 from the Caribbean to Montreal. During the climb under Center Control, we received further clearance to climb to 21,000 feet. I was sitting in the right seat, acting as a PNF, so I read back the clearance.

As in any phase of flight, a pilot should always be watching in front of the airplane for weather and surrounding airplane traffic. As far as traffic, we use the aircraft's navigation display to observe the Traffic Alert and Collision Avoidance System (TCAS), which displays where airplanes are situated in flight around the aircraft, the direction they are heading, and the altitude.

The airspace we were flying in and transitioning from one control center to the other is extremely busy, with airplanes flying south to Caribbean destinations and flying back up north to Canada. At 19,000 feet in the climb, I noticed on my navigation display (ND) that there was another airplane at 21,000 feet, which was not alarming if this airplane was going the same northern direction as we were or on a perpendicular track, as that would not cause any issues. But that was not the case—this airplane was heading south and straight towards us on the same track we were on.

"Center, confirm Air Transat 424 we are cleared to FL 210?" I asked.

"Affirm, Air Transat 424. Climb FL 210 and contact next controller on 130.75."

"Roger, switching to 130.75. Just to inform you, we have traffic position approximately 40 miles north at Level 210, heading southbound, same track."

"Ok, TSC424 contact next controller!"

We were right in the transition zone between both airspaces.

I switched frequency to next control airspace, but good luck putting a word in. The controller was extremely busy, and pilots kept stepping on each other, jamming the radio frequency, until the controller told everyone not to transmit unless contacted.

While I was calling Center, my colleague reduced our rate of climb, and although cleared to 21,000, we slowly climbed to 20,000 until the airplane north of us flew right overhead of our position at 21,000 feet, heading southbound at the altitude we were cleared to. A 1000 feet separation was the minimum altitude required between both airplanes.

Flying the airplane first is always top priority. Always be aware of the traffic around you and where they are heading. Situational awareness is key.

FIRST ENGINE FAILURE

Hurricane Irma was approaching the Caribbean in September 2017, and my airline was planning rescue flights to bring back Canadians who were vacationing down south. I received a call from Crew Scheduling the evening of September 5 and was assigned a flight the next day to Punta Cana. The mission was to fly an empty B737 airplane down south and bring back as many passengers as possible before the storm was to make landfall the next day.

I had tickets for a concert I'd been waiting so long to go to on the evening of the flight, so I swapped flights with a colleague supervisor whose return flight was earlier than mine. Instead of flying to Punta Cana, I was now assigned to the flight to Samaná, which was in the northern part of the Dominican Republic. With an earlier arrival time, I would be able to go to the concert.

I joined my FO in the crew room, who recently joined the airline six months prior. I was looking forward to flying with him since the last time I saw him was during the simulator evaluation during his interview process.

Once at the airplane, we met the cabin crew and I gave the captain briefing. I then proceeded to perform the exterior walk-around and my FO went on to perform the cockpit preparation, as he would be the PF on this leg of the flight.

Since we didn't have any passengers on this portion of the flight, it didn't take too long before we pushed back. We had some light to moderate turbulence from approximately 10,000 feet up to 21,000, and then above that altitude we cleared the cloud layer and entered smooth air. I looked at the flight instruments and engine parameters; everything was working flawlessly until we climbed through 26,000 feet. What we heard was a sound—*BANG*—as if we hit something. Then suddenly the whole fuselage started vibrating and shaking as if we were flying through hail or a sandstorm. I had never heard or felt an airplane produce such a sound and vibration.

I looked at the left-wing, as this was the rattled side; I had a feeling something hit our wing. Half a second later, I glanced at the engine instruments and saw the left engine parameters indicate that this engine failed and had sustained severe damage.

With only one engine now producing thrust on only one side, the airplane created very noticeable yaw, which required precise handling of the airplane. Also, we had to stop the climb, as we were not able to continue to the cleared altitude of 38,000 feet.

The main goal was to first control the airplane; second, secure the failed engine through a memory drill/checklist; and third, inform Air Traffic Control once that was completed. Aviate, Navigate, and Communicate.

In simulator training, pilots mostly practice engine failures during takeoff and on the go-around, and on occasion, in some phases of training, in cruise at a high level. These are all predictable since pilots expect them to happen. But in real life, it is different—the element of surprise is present, which in our case was the engine failing at 26,000 feet.

Just like the crew on US Airways Flight 1549, where double engine failure occurred right after takeoff, the element of surprise was there. The good thing is that the engine failure drill on the B737 is straightforward and enabled us to deal with this malfunction regardless of what altitude we were going through.

Once this situation occurred in flight, we were able to switch right away into a "mission-minded" mode, to deal with this malfunction just as we would in training in the simulator.

As we were on descent, returning to Montreal's airport, I was thinking to myself for the first time, after all these years flying jets, I had one engine holding us in the air. Since at that moment we did not know what caused the failure on the left engine, as a safety precaution I kept my ND showing all the airports in our flight path, in case we would experience any problems with the second engine.

I briefed the FD that we were returning to Montreal-Trudeau Airport, although he already knew something was wrong with the airplane. The approach and landing were performed well, and once we landed, emergency vehicles inspected the aircraft before it was towed to the airline's hangar.

Every flight is a lesson for a pilot, from the smooth and uneventful flights to the ones with sudden malfunctions. It is important to be vigilant and stay focused during any flight. Expect the unexpected, and when things go bad, first take a couple of seconds to analyze what's going on, relax, and fly the airplane before doing anything else. Know your airplane inside out and be proficient with its systems and memory drills so that if things do not go as planned, you will be ready.

BACK ON THE AIRBUS A330

In May 2018, a position opened at Flight Ops for a supervisor on the Airbus A330. The B737 fleet was being reduced, and the A330 team needed one more supervisor to assist the chief pilot with the twenty-airplane fleet.

I was happy to be part of the B737 team and help introduce the new type to the airline, help ferry the airplanes at the beginning of the operations, build the training program, help the B737 successful operations, and train new supervisors that joined the team in the past.

I was looking forward to the opportunity to join the A330 team, be part of its operations, and go back into long-range and oceanic flying, across the Atlantic and to Europe—which has always been the type of flying I enjoy. It has always been special to witness the sunrise over the Atlantic, sipping coffee at 40,000 feet, and traveling at Mach .81.

Mid-Atlantic on the A330, July 2019.

1000 feet separation over the Atlantic on the NAT.

A beautiful view from the office A330

I was incredibly grateful to be awarded the supervisor position on the A330 and looked forward to the simulator, line training, and mastering the airplane. The A330 was a senior airplane, which in airline jargon means there are many senior captains and first officers assigned to this airplane. Therefore, since I was going to instruct, test, and supervise pilots on this type of airplane, I had to make sure to be well proficient on it.

I had to do a complete initial training, as the last time I flew the airplane had been a while ago and I wasn't current on it anymore. The good thing was that the initial training comprised of eighteen simulator sessions, which is plenty to get familiarized with an airplane.

Since Boeing and Airbus have a different philosophy when operating and dealing with malfunctions, once all the online system training was completed, the first manual I reviewed was the SOPs. The big difference between the A330 and the B737 is that the A330 has a system called Electronic Centralized Aircraft Monitoring (ECAM), which monitors aircraft functions and relays them to the pilots. It also produces messages detailing failures and, in certain cases, lists procedures to undertake to correct the problem. Also, the A330 is a fly-by-wire aircraft, where the philosophy of flying the airplane is different than the B737.

The B737 uses a conventional control wheel, column, and pedals that are linked mechanically to hydraulic power control units commanding the primary flight control surfaces. On the Airbus A330, instead of a control wheel, the pilot uses a sidestick to control the aircraft. The flight controls are electronically controlled and hydraulically activated. The aircraft's numerous computers ensure the airplane is always maintained in a safe flight envelope.

The flight simulator has very advanced, extremely realistic technology and flies just like the airplane. The outside visuals are very realistic in the simulator. For example, one can see cars driving over bridges when coming into land or when at the gate; airport trucks can be seen maneuvering on the ramp. The simulator can also simulate all kinds of weather conditions, where pilots can experience wind shear conditions, icy runways, thunderstorms, heavy rain, and crosswind landings, to name a few.

My simulator partner and I were both progressing very well, and our last two training sessions and final flight test were conducted in the simulator training center in London, UK, since the one in Montreal was fully booked. The last session was the touch-and-go, where lots of hand-flying was performed. With the fly-by-wire and sidestick system of the Airbus A330, the airplane has excellent handling characteristics, requiring very little and gentle inputs from the pilots when hand-flying.

The final simulator test was completed on July 14, 2018, and the next stage was to complete line indoctrination training, which consisted of forty flight hours with an instructor followed by a final line check.

My first line training flight was on July 20, from YUL to CDG, on aircraft A330-200 model C-GUFR. For this departure I was fortunate to have my brother take beautiful pictures of the takeoff. Right next to Montreal-Trudeau Airport, near Runway 06R, is the Jacques-de-Lesseps Park. This park is so close to the runway that people can see aircraft take off and land. Even the engine vibration can be felt on the ground as the airplanes take off.

It felt great as I taxied the airplane, knowing my little brother was just on the other side of the airport fence taking pictures.

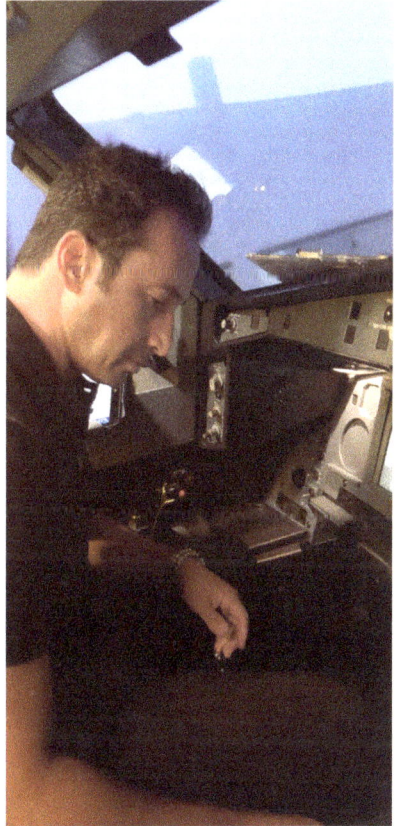

A330 simulator training, London, UK.
July 2018

Nir taking some great shots.

First flight of line Indoctrination as Captain/Supervisor; A330-200 C-GUFR lIning up on Runway 06R, YUL to CDG.

The A330 is a magical airplane to fly. The flight deck is huge and has lots of storage everywhere. You can comfortably stand and stretch your legs during a flight. The aircraft's performance for takeoff is never an issue, due to its massive and powerful engines. The weight and balance envelope and calculations have never been an issue on any of my flights, due to the aircraft's big performance envelope.

Climbing early in the flight to the high levels is rarely an issue, not like other airplanes that need to burn fuel before slowly crawling to 36,000 feet and higher. Also, while in cruise, since the engines are so far back and with silent air conditioning fans, the cockpit is a very quiet place for the pilots to work, so a ten-hour flight is very comfortable.

At cruise altitude, pilots can remove their headsets and communicate with Air Traffic Control by using a handset and a speaker, and they can talk to one another in the flight deck in a normal tone of voice.

Since the aircraft has no control yoke in front of the pilots, there is lots of room in front of your knees, giving not only ample legroom but also a clear view of all the flight instruments. Instead of the control wheel, on the Airbus A330 and some other Airbus models, pilots have access to a stowable tray that can be used to put checklists, manuals, and a meal tray.

Landing the airplane is a lot of fun. Despite its size, the approach speed is normal and like any other jet airplanes, making the approach and landings easy. The important thing to remember is that the airplane will not slow down and descend at the same time. It's an airplane with a 197-foot wingspan. It loves to fly, so good planning for the approach and being stabilized early will make a pilot's job easy; otherwise a go-around will be necessary. The airplane has a lot of inertia, so small corrections are needed to let the airplane first react, and overcontrolling will make it very difficult to remain stabilized on the final approach.

The braking system on the airplane is impeccable even on contaminated surfaces. Also, the combination of the autobrake system, ground spoilers, and reverse thrust produces excellent deceleration performance, leading to impressive short landing distances.

I can go on and on about this airplane and how much I enjoy flying it; some might think I am an aircraft salesman for the manufacturer! Overall, it is an impressive airplane and a pleasure to fly.

For the final line check, I had the opportunity to fly with the chief pilot to Marseille. We had fun having a day off from the office and having dinner together in Europe.

Short final Runway 24R in YUL, Montreal, on Airbus A330-300.

EXPECT THE UNEXPECTED

In July 2019, we were operating a scheduled flight from Lisbon to Toronto on aircraft C-GUBC, an A330-200 which was on my yearly captain line check.

The flight was routine: seven and a half hours, a normal departure from Lisbon, smooth air, and no weather in the cruise portion of the flight. We did expect some thunderstorms and build-up weather upon arrival to Toronto, but with no delays. We were cleared for the STAR approach and didn't have to deviate around weather, as most of it was located to the west of the airport.

"Flaps 1," I called as we were now on initial radar vectors to Runway 23, maintaining a speed of 220 knots.

"Speed checked. Flaps 1," my colleague replied.

"Flaps 2," I called, as now we were established on the final approach and tracking the localizer system of the ILS.

Extending the wing flaps and slats increases the camber or curvature of the wing, raising the maximum lift coefficient. Doing that allows the aircraft to generate the required lift while decelerating to a lower speed, which is being reduced during the approach, reducing the minimum speed (known as stall speed) at which the aircraft will safely maintain flight. Increasing the camber also increases the wing drag, which in this case will help to decelerate the aircraft during the approach and allow it to slow to final landing speed.

"Speed check," replied the check pilot, and he selected the flaps to position two, which resulted in the ECAM system displaying two different flight control faults.

We had a few seconds to see if we could reset the fault, but we both knew that we would be going around very shortly—which we did.

"Go-around flaps," I called, and set maximum thrust.

We went from seven and a half hours of calm and uneventful flight to pulling up from the approach, going around and getting busy. We climbed to a safe altitude, then proceeded with our respective duties.

While going around and flying at 3000 feet—a low altitude—the engines were consuming a lot of fuel. Not only that, but the airport had to close Runway 23 due to a bird strike and the requirement for a runway inspection due to a previous landing aircraft. Now all traffic was being directed to land on Runway 24L, and with weather approaching fast from the west and with only one useable runway, we were prompted to return on the approach quickly.

The next few minutes of our workload were extremely busy and demanding. We had to complete all checklists, perform the landing calculations, brief the flight attendants, make a passenger announcement, and brief the approach. In a situation like this, my task was only to fly the airplane since I was going to perform the approach, but the PM had a much higher workload. The PM was extremely busy, performing many tasks while communicating with Air Traffic Control and assisting the PF.

We were back on the approach and landing was completed with no further issues. The lesson learned here is that a flight can go perfectly smooth with no issues, then in the last few minutes have a busy flight deck. Always be ready!

CHAPTER 9

✈

AMBASSADOR TO AVIATION

I always had the desire to give back to aviation and to be an ambassador for the airline I was working for. Therefore, I had the opportunity to take part in some rewarding and fun projects for Air Transat, such as

going on roadshows to career fairs, being in commercials for the airline, photoshoots for advertising, and one of my favorite things, spending time with a children foundation that came to visit the airline's headquarters.

There are many personal reasons I wanted to be part of these projects. I have always considered myself lucky to be in my dream profession, so I wanted to give back. Also, children can sometimes have difficulties deciding what they would like to do when they grow up, so the opportunity to show them our airplanes and the inside of a cockpit could incite the possibility of a career in aviation.

A fun hangar visit and tour of the Airbus A310.

Going back to Perimeter, training pilots was gratifying to me, as I was able to give back to the industry but most of all share my knowledge with pilots learning to fly the Metro. I have over 6000 hours of flight time on the Metro II aircraft and lots of knowledge and passion to share with the pilots of the airline that gave me my first aviation job.

Going on roadshows with the HR team and my colleagues was our way of promoting Air Transat and sharing our passion for our company and the industry. To have a chance to guide and meet future aviation employees in their application process and aspiring youth who are curious about the industry and to be there as a resource to answer any questions on a personal level was rewarding.

Today, the Internet has a great deal of information regarding the aviation industry, but the chance to speak face-to-face with an airline pilot, an airline mechanic, or a talent acquisition Human Resources representative is a great opportunity that wasn't available when I was in flight school.

I had the chance to join the airline's team at many airshows, the Manitoba Aviation conference, and the career expo for the Canadian Air cadets in Ottawa.

One event that I enjoyed attending was in October 2018, where we had the opportunity to be at the Royal Canadian Air Cadets career expo in Ottawa. The Cadets is a Canadian national youth program for young individuals aged twelve to nineteen. Under the authority of the National Defense Act, the program is administered by the Canadian Forces and funded through the Department of National Defense.

Bromont Air Show, May 31, 2019.

Most of the Cadet training takes place at the local squadron during the regular school year and a percentage of Cadets are selected for summer training courses at various Cadet training centers located across Canada. The Air Cadet program has the gliders and flying scholarships offered to those who qualify. Many commercial and airline pilots began their careers as Air Cadets. I had the opportunity to spend one summer in the Cadets; I greatly enjoyed my experience but did not take part in the flying scholarships.

There were thousands of Air Cadets attending this convention, and we had the great opportunity to meet and speak to many Cadets who were curious about airline flying, flight schools, and overall had questions regarding a career in aviation.

There are many ways to pursue a career as an airline pilot, aircraft mechanic, flight attendant, or any other aviation profession. There isn't one route someone should choose over another. But with that in mind, I've often been asked about things like which flight school to go to, whether a university or college degree is mandatory to become an airline pilot, whether flight clubs are better than flight colleges, the costs, how to get loans, which companies to apply to after graduating, what regions have the most opportunities to get your first job in aviation, what the pros and cons are of being an airline pilot versus business aviation or flying cargo, and so on.

There are excellent colleges in Canada offering complete flight training programs, which include the PPL, CPL, multi-engine IFR, and ATPL programs. With that, students can also obtain a college diploma. For this program, a student loan will be required.

Another option is obtaining the PPL, CPL, and multi-engine IFR license through a flight center, where funds should be available in advance by the student pilot.

I believe the Air Cadets is a great opportunity, and a flying career in the military is an excellent option as well.

There are also flight colleges in Canada subsidized by the government. It's best to contact these schools for more information about programs and admission. It's also important to go visit these schools when there are open houses. Do not get discouraged if you are not accepted on the first try. I've heard of some pilots only getting in a specific college on the third try.

There are pros and cons in any route one chooses to obtain flying lessons, so it's up to each person to evaluate them. The key is to research the schools and ask as many questions as you can about the programs and student loans. Also, it is important to be in a full-time program with no major gaps between flights, licenses, and ratings. Learning to fly and a positive progression happens with repetition and practice. I would not recommend allowing for major gaps between flights and courses. Going on that FAM flight as soon as possible at the local flying club is highly recommended. It will give you an idea right from the start of what flying is all about.

In April 2018, we headed to Winnipeg for the Manitoba Career Fair, where we had a chance to sponsor the event and meet our passengers from Central and Western Canada and also meet airline professionals who had come to talk to us about our company.

We had the opportunity to give a presentation in an auditorium and to talk about our airline, our career progress, what it is like to be an airline pilot, our schedule, the type of flying we did, and the hiring process.

Career Expo, October 14, 2018.

After the conference, while in Winnipeg I took the opportunity to visit Perimeter Aviation and say hello to past colleagues. Although it had been many years since I was at Perimeter, it felt like I was back at home. It was nice to see some pilots and mechanics I had worked with in the past.

Manitoba Aviation Conference, April 2018.

Another project I had the chance to participate in was meeting new air traffic controllers who came for a visit at the airline's headquarters. It was a yearly planned event where new and experienced controllers had a chance to meet an airline pilot and talk about our profession and how we operate our aircraft. It was also a chance for them to see the cockpit and all the navigation and communication equipment we use in flight.

On the day of the visit, I greeted the eight air traffic controllers, who arrived at the airline's HQ. We had an Airbus A330 out on the ramp available for the visit. I had the chance to talk about the airplane and some of its components, and then we went up to the flight deck. It was an opportunity to show our pilot workstation, how we communicated with the controllers, the automation system of the airplane, its navigation equipment, and many other components of the flight deck.

It was a lot of fun to share stories and talk about our profession. We also talked about what controllers can do for pilots to make their job easier, and the same from the pilot's perspective, as well as emergencies, airplane performances, and some regulations. Then we talked about our careers and how we got into our profession.

I enjoyed the two visits I had with the air traffic controllers. I always knew the selection process and training program for air traffic controllers is very rigorous and demanding and that it requires great skills and aptitude to succeed in the program. I found a lot of similarities between pilots and controllers, as it takes a certain type of personality to be able to take huge responsibilities day in and day out.

When flying into heavy-traffic airspace during a busy period, I am always impressed at how the controllers manage many airplanes at the same time, sequencing them into the arrival corridor to an airport. It is very neat to hear the calm and composed voice of the controller on the radio handling all these airplanes into one or two runways while the tower controllers are launching and receiving landing airplanes. It is impressive, and I have great respect and admiration for their profession and the people who control our airspace.

The last project I took part in for the airline was in January of 2020. A flight attendant colleague and I were guests on a TV series that had a culinary competition where candidates were eliminated on every episode until one chef would win the final competition.

The airline was offering a prize on the fourth episode, so we announced the prize the remaining chefs had won.

At the last minute of filming, all the finalists were standing in front of a long kitchen counter between the head chef judge and the show announcer. The host of the show informed the candidates that they would be heading to another city in Quebec to film the next episode, but just before she announced the location, she informed everyone that there were two guests on the show. That was when my colleague and I came out on set.

As we walked on set, I noticed the nine chef candidates staring at us in shock, not understanding why there was a pilot and flight attendant in uniform on a cooking show. Then once we were in our designated position, we announced to the candidates that they would be heading to New Orleans to film the next episode.

They were ecstatic to hear the news, as many of them had never been to this amazing city before and now they had the chance to cook and film in New Orleans. They were all cheering and hugging each other with joy, and we were happy to be part of this special moment.

On TV set, April 2020.

I enjoyed and am grateful to take part in many of these projects and events throughout my career. I had the chance to meet amazing people, to represent the airline, and to give back to the industry I am extremely passionate about. I look forward to many more future projects.

CHAPTER 10

✈

THREE THINGS EVERY PILOT MUST KNOW

Pilots need a lot of knowledge and skill to operate airplanes safely and efficiently. You can't excel in only one subject, but instead you need to be good at many things.

Here are the three fundamental rules that helped me through my pilot training and airline career:

1. Aviate, navigate, and communicate—always in that order.

2. Attitude plus power equals performance.

3. Be one step ahead.

The most important lesson any pilot must learn and apply from the very beginning of their pilot training and for the rest of their career is to aviate, navigate, and communicate—in that order, always, especially when in an emergency or an unusual situation.

The top priority—always—is to aviate. To aviate means to fly the airplane by using the flight controls and flight instruments to control the airplane's attitude, airspeed, and altitude. Next is to navigate, which is knowing where you are and where you're going. Finally, as appropriate, communicate by talking to ATC or someone outside the airplane on the radio.

Aviate, navigate, and communicate—seems simple, but it's easy to forget when a pilot gets busy or distracted in the flight deck. An example of a failure to aviate is when Flight 401, an Eastern Airlines Lockheed L-1011, crashed in December 1972. The entire crew was single-mindedly focused on the malfunction of a landing gear position indicator light. No one from the flight crew was left to keep the airplane in the air as it headed towards the ground in the Florida Everglades. Any one of the crew could have detected the descent and taken control of the aircraft.

Nothing is more important than flying the airplane and keeping it flying safely. Everything else is secondary. No matter what happens, control the aircraft first. If there are two pilots, then one pilot can be tasked with only flying the airplane and the other can be doing everything else.

The second fundamental and critical lesson in aviation is attitude plus power equals performance. In other words, an aircraft's performance is the product of attitude and power. Performance is expressed in terms of airspeed, altitude, rate of climb or descent, or other criteria. If either attitude or power is changed, a change in performance will result.

Whether it's a Cessna 152, an FA-18, or an A330, your combination of power setting and angle of attack will determine what the aircraft will do. That's been true since the Wright brothers' first flight. It's the way airplanes fly, and it's the first lesson in flying and the thing to remember when your airplane does not appear to be flying.

Finally, always be one step ahead. As a student pilot or an airline pilot, being one step ahead, thinking, and preparing for what's next will keep you ahead of the game. Don't jump several steps ahead. Instead, focus on completing your current task and thinking about what do to next.

Here's an example: You are in an Airbus A330, taxiing in Lisbon, Portugal, heading to Toronto Pearson. You can't be thinking about your oceanic clearance at that point; it's something you will eventually work on getting. You must complete the Before Takeoff Checklist first. Then, you are expecting a call from the FD confirming that the cabin is secure. Next, as you approach the active runway you are confirming that all checklists are completed before accepting a takeoff clearance. Then, it's time to get the weather radar on in case there is weather on departure. You are airborne, passing 10,000 feet, and the Climb Checklist is complete. You then call company operations with the departure and ETA to destination times. Now you are thinking about calling the Oceanic Control on another frequency and getting the oceanic clearance. Later in the flight, you will review the airport charts and brief the approach way before the Top of Descent point. In case Air Traffic Control will initiate an early descent, you will already be ahead and approach briefing will be completed in time.

What I'm getting at is that by being a pilot who is always consistent and who is always one step ahead of the game, you will always be safe and operationally on the right path. You will anticipate things before they happen by being one step ahead.

If anything happens, you ensure the airplane is under control first and then deal with the malfunction or abnormality calmly and methodically. This mindset has helped me throughout my career.

Now how about getting that dream flying job and preparing for the interview process. Is there a magic formula?

HOW TO PREPARE FOR THE PILOT INTERVIEW

Pilots will go through many interviews throughout their careers. Some pilots will be lucky and do one or two interviews in their whole career if they were able to stay with the same airline and company for many years, even retiring with them. Others will go through many interviews throughout their careers if the companies they worked for go bankrupt or stop operations or if they decide to pursue better and bigger opportunities with other airlines.

Interviews can be a challenging process and stressful procedure for any pilot regardless of flight experience. Since I've been through a few of them myself and also been part of interview panels for a couple of airlines, I'd like to share some of my knowledge on how to prepare for that big interview.

There are many interview prep books out there, and the Internet is full of information about this important subject that pilots have easy access to. Therefore, this chapter is more specific to my personal observations and the lessons I learned through both failed and successful attempts.

Let's begin.

First, know as much as you can about the airline you are applying to: its history, route structure, culture, mission statement, clientele, revenues, key personnel, and most importantly, their interview style and hiring process. Some airlines conduct a very technical interview process to see the pilot's knowledge. Others have an approach to learn about the candidate's personality and see if they will fit well in the company's culture. Some airlines will have psychological exams and simulator evaluations as well. Therefore, getting all that information in advance and catering your prep for that style of interview is a must.

Once you have all that information, it is time to prepare a plan for the interview with a specific deadline so that everything will be ready before the interview date. This could mean purchasing and preparing clothing attire for the interview, getting all paperwork organized (i.e., pilot logbook), booking a haircut/style appointment, visiting the address where the interview will take place to be familiar with the route you will take on the interview date, and so on. Without a plan, you may risk forgetting an important item.

Brush up on your IFR regulations and make sure you know your aircraft limitations and systems well, as some candidates could be asked about the airplane they currently fly, especially if you are applying with an airline that has the same type of airplane you're currently flying. It will not look good if you don't know your airplane well. The more experience you have, the more demanding you can expect the interview team to be for good answers.

To be able to answer well with good examples to any questions that might be asked, during the preparation go over your career to date and write down notes about events that you have experienced, such as important challenging flights and the decisions you made, whether good or bad. Going through your pilot logbook is a good way to recall those flights. If you know good examples and stories to share and how to back up your answers with the interview panel, the answers will come out genuine, honest, and authentic instead of robotic or too well-rehearsed. You want to be natural when you give your answers. The more recent examples and events shared in an interview, the better. Remember the interview panel interviews thousands of candidates, so they have experience. Be ready to answer questions about mistakes or errors you have made and don't use being a perfectionist as a weakness. We've heard that one too many times.

Do not try too hard to impress; it could come out fake. Use your previous experience and what you have done up to this point to prove your abilities, knowledge, and qualities. Actions speak louder than words.

The interview process could be very demanding and stressful. Therefore, being nervous is natural, and it's ok to be. Someone way too comfortable could come across as overconfident. The key is to relax, listen well to the question asked, and take a couple of seconds to compose your answer.

Practice, practice, and practice delivering your answers so that they come out naturally. The best crowd you can practice with includes a family member or a friend who will be able to critique you well. Filming your practice interview is a good idea. The interview panel is assessing many things about you while in the interview, not just your answers to the questions. Will you fit well in the company's culture? Are you trainable? Do you have good communication skills? Are you dependable and honest? Do you make good eye contact and smile? What would it be like to go on a five-day pairing to Europe with you, and so on?

There are hundreds of different questions an airline interview panel can ask a candidate, but responses to the following questions have to be well prepared, as it is highly likely these will be asked, and the panel will take the opportunity to get to know you through them. Remember if you don't say something about yourself, the panel will never know, so be ready for the following questions:

1. Tell us about yourself and your career path to date.

2. Why do you want to work for this airline?

3. What are your strengths and weaknesses?

   Note: If you answer that being a perfectionist is your weakness, guess what? So have the other 80% of the candidates. If you want to stand out, have a good answer to that question and what you have been doing to correct or improve yourself.

4. Tell us about a mistake you have made as a pilot.

5. Have you applied with other airlines?

6. There are many good candidates for the position, what makes you stand out from the rest?

7. Where do you see yourself in the next five or ten years?

Now, companies that use the simulator as part of the evaluation consider this stage particularly important. If the simulator type is not an airplane you have flown before, which is mostly the case, there are a few important preparations to make.

Familiarize yourself as much as possible with the cockpit layout and all switches and knobs. Be aware of the systems on board (i.e., autothrust, flight director, glass cockpit, or basic instrumentation). There are many videos available online that can be a great tool to familiarize yourself with the cockpit layout and equipment.

Review and be very familiar with the simulator flight profile if provided by the airline. If the possibility to rent simulator time before the evaluation is available, then that is highly recommended. Flying skills are not the only skills being evaluated in the simulator evaluation, but also personality, IFR knowledge, communication skills, CRM, stress management decision-making, and much more. From the moment you step into the simulator center until the moment you leave, you are being evaluated.

Image and grooming are especially important. You will represent the airline in uniform, so looking neat and professional is key. Showing up on time is obvious but must be reminded. Arrive at the interview location and present yourself a few minutes early. Everyone you meet or talk to can be part of your evaluation process; never let your guard down or get too comfortable until you leave the premises.

Do not dwell on mistakes; remember to smile and most of all relax! All the hard work will pay off!

After push back in YYZ B737-800 NG.

IT'S A SMALL INDUSTRY

The airline industry in Canada compared to the United States and Europe is relatively small. There are two big major airlines in the country. Once these airlines go through a major hiring period, this leads to open flying positions in the smaller regional carriers.

Airlines will usually publish the minimum experience required to apply, which is considerably low most of the time, but that varies with the state of the industry during a particular period. When the industry is thriving and major airlines are hiring, pilots with more experience will be hired before those with or close to the minimum requirements.

Experience is very important to have, and the more flight hours someone has, particularly with jets or turboprops, the better. Also, with some airlines an applicant that has on-type flight experience and is still current on that airplane has an advantage over others.

But experience is not everything. Internal references from a company pilot or employee of an airline that a candidate is applying to could sometimes be much more helpful than flight experience.

Most of the time, airlines have a limited number of open pilot positions and an overwhelming number of applicants. The proof of that was during COVID-19. Thousands of highly experienced pilots were applying to very few open positions available. Those who were able to find a job during that difficult time were the ones who had internal references or knew someone in the airline. This happens not only with pilots or in aviation, but in many other professions as well. Again, this is not the only way to get an interview with an airline, but it is always helpful to have good contacts. Pilots are not only hired for their flying skills but, more importantly, for their personality and attitude. Therefore, someone already working for the airline with good standings who can say that Joe or Shannon, for example, will fit very well in the company's culture will go a long way compared to the unknown applicant. The aviation industry can be very small sometimes; despite living in a big country, many pilots know each other. Someone can be a chief pilot in one airline and, many years later, apply somewhere with another company where the person responsible for hiring could've once been under their supervision. Also, it is very important to never burn any bridges with any airline or colleague as a pilot's reputation is as important as their experience.

I have crossed paths throughout my career with some of my schoolmates; we'd ended up working for the same airline many years after graduating. When I was nineteen, I had a friend I used to work out with, but we eventually lost touch after I moved to Winnipeg. Fifteen years later, we happened to meet in the crew room, discovering we were going on a flight together to Europe on the Airbus A310. At another time, as I was meeting the outbound A310 pilots in Amsterdam on the jetway I caught up with a pilot who mentioned that his girlfriend was my first instructor on my first flight on the Cessna back in 1997. As I said before, aviation is a small industry!

Although solid flight experience will help a pilot in their profession when dealing with various situations and on day-to-day operations, as well as getting promotions within the airline to highly skilled positions, what gets job opportunities is having solid contacts in the industry. Experience alone will not be sufficient to help obtain that call for the interview.

Lastly, just as important as references and experience is luck. Being in the right place, at the right time, and with the right people—those willing to open doors—can help some pilots progress and get new opportunities in their profession. Stay positive, humble, optimistic and things will happen for you!

LONG HAUL INTERNATIONAL FLYING AND JET LAG

The techniques I am going to share are personal and work for me as far as flying internationally. It's worth mentioning that each pilot or flight attendant might have their own ways to deal with jet lag.

First, the type of flying I have done in the last few years has been from North America to Europe, which, in my airline, varies from seven to eleven hours on average, depending on the departure and destination. These flights involve one takeoff and one landing, and once in Europe, most often pilots head to a hotel for a layover. The other type of flying is what's called a "turn," where a typical route would be a flight from Canada to, for example, Cancun, Mexico and then right back to Canada on the same day. This duty day, which can last from eight to twelve hours, includes two takeoffs and two landings.

The latter eliminates the issue of jet lag, but I find this type of duty day to be more tiring and demanding than a one-leg flight to Europe or from Europe back to Canada. Besides the fact that it entails two approaches and two takeoffs in one day, with a short stop in between, pilots usually have to deal with the same weather, turbulence, and airspaces traveled flying south as they do flying back north. A flight to Europe, on the other hand, does not have these challenges, but then again that's the beauty of working in an airline—pilots can choose what type of flying they prefer to do.

Most departures to Europe from Canada and the United States occur in the evening hours, as all air traffic has an eastbound flow at night and westbound flow during the day. Most of the flights I have been scheduled on the Airbus A310 and A330 to Europe from Canada had departure times between 7:00 p.m. and 11:30 p.m., when most people are asleep or heading to bed.

A pilot will typically show up to work an hour and a half to two hours before their flight, then fly an average of eight to ten hours to Europe, and then it's another hour to two before they arrive at a hotel, which altogether adds up to a long workday—not to mention, you will witness nightfall and sunrise in one flight. Therefore, living a healthy lifestyle and managing rest well are key if a pilot wants to maintain a long and enjoyable flying career.

Now, many times I get asked if pilots are allowed to stay wherever they fly to, and the answer is yes. There are many rest period rules that airlines need to respect when scheduling a flight. Flight crews will usually have at least a twenty-four hour layover in Europe before flying back. The rest period rules have recently changed, and now pilots get even more rest and better work conditions. Those who hold good seniority in an airline may get lucky with a forty-eight hour layover at their destination.

If my flight to Paris is scheduled, for example, to depart Toronto at 8:00 p.m., then on that day I will plan to wake up early in the morning, say at 7:00 or 8:00 a.m. After waking up, I will take the opportunity to pack my suitcase, prepare my flight bag, and get my uniform ready. I'll try to keep my daily errands free so as not to tire myself too much. I will plan a workout that day and, most importantly, try to fit in a two-hour or longer nap in the afternoon, which is the key to being well-rested for the flight.

I always plan a time to start getting ready and a time to leave the house, with a target to be at the airport at least two hours before the flight departure, although an hour or an hour twenty is what is required by most airlines. The earlier you show up at the airport, the better.

Meal choices for pilots have come around a lot through the years, as there has been more effort to keep higher standards. But most of the time I bring my meals on my flights. I stick to foods such as salads and light meals that do not upset my stomach. For example, foods like beans, onions, and certain fruits and vegetables could cause digestion problems. I would stay away from heavy foods like bread and pasta. You want to eat healthy foods that will give you energy, keep you awake, and not put you to sleep.

Now that I live in a big city, I always do a final road traffic update before leaving my house to make sure I will not get stuck. Depending on the time of day and what is going on in the city, I sometimes take the subway rather than drive.

I am a coffee lover and drink one cup a day on average. I find it beneficial to stay energized during flight and drink at least 1.5 liters or more of water on an average flight of seven to ten hours. Staying hydrated in flight and throughout the pairing is especially important. Also, I find keeping the cockpit temperature on the cool side helps keep me energized, as having a hot cockpit temperature can fatigue the body.

By the time I arrive at the hotel in Europe, I have been up for more than fourteen hours, so I am tired. Since most of the hotels we stay at are well situated and have small fridges in their rooms, I usually head out to the grocery stores to buy some basics food for my stay and return flight, such as water, yogurt, nuts, or pre-made salads. Once my groceries are done, then it's nap time until dinner.

There were summers I would fly to Europe four to five times per month on average, which is very demanding on anyone, regardless of how fit you are or how well you eat. The profession requires not only to fly an airplane but many other things, such as managing rest and a healthy lifestyle, preparing for recurrent training, keeping up on the company and technical memos, and managing your personal life. Considering this, time management and planning are essential. What someone does in their free time will greatly impact their ability to work and their career altogether. It comes down to planning and being well organized.

Once I am overseas, for example, in Europe, I will adjust myself to the local time and not stay in my home time zone in Canada. Some will disagree and remain in the time zone they live in, which is not wrong; it just does not work for me. I will try to go to sleep in Europe at the normal local time, say 10:00 or 11:00 p.m. How long I remain asleep varies: sometimes I can stay asleep without waking up for six hours, and other times I can only sleep for two. Using earplugs helps me sleep well; I am a light sleeper and can wake up to any small noise, so this helps me tremendously.

Many times, the hotel's hallways or outside the hotel can be noisy; getting woken up is the worst thing that can happen, as falling back to sleep can sometimes be impossible. Usually, hotels that have crews will give rooms on the quieter side of the floor, away from the elevators, but if that service is not available, you should make the request.

I will not work out or do any sports overseas, as I find that the body is already fatigued due to the jet lag, so pushing it further is not necessary. I am also against sleeping pills and melatonin. I believe that sleep should be natural, and if I end up waking up in the middle of the night, then reading a book or magazine will help me fall back to sleep. Avoid an iPad or iPhone if you are trying to fall asleep.

But sometimes even with all the tricks in my bag, I cannot get a long, decent sleep. Waking up at 1:00 or 2:00 a.m. and staying awake for a few hours does happen occasionally. The good thing is, though, that the return flight back to North America happens during the day, which means staying in the daylight hours can help you remain energized.

Staying healthy and stress-free is important, and to have a long and healthy career, a pilot must do whatever they can to maintain that lifestyle. Our profession depends on our medical license being valid, and once a pilot loses their privileges for whatever reason, it can be complicated to get it back.

It's important to have at least two alarms set up, on top of a wake-up call from the hotel. I would have one set up at the low volume so as not to get startled when it rings and the second one set up at high volume in case I miss the first one. You do not want to oversleep and have the whole crew wait for you in the crew bus. That's a little embarrassing.

I typically wake up at least an hour before the scheduled wake-up time and head out for a good breakfast, usually at the hotel, bringing my iPad along so that I can review all the flight folder documents. Once that is all done, I head back to the room, and since I packed everything the night before, all I need to do is to put my uniform on and take a good walk around the room to make sure I didn't forget anything and to organize things as well. Always make sure important items are not forgotten, like your cell phone, licenses, passport, airport security pass, and wallet.

Jet lag and long-haul flights can be tiresome, so they require good planning and managing by aircrew. But a pro of that type of flying is the opportunity to see beautiful places around the world. My favorite thing to do on layovers, in my free time, is to go to the beach if there is one, visit museums, go shopping, and sightsee. I love good cuisine, and enjoying delicious local food is a must. Also, the opportunity to have dinner with the crew is something I enjoy very much, as it's a chance to spend time with and get to know my colleagues.

For me, the opportunity to fly to beautiful places all over the world is amazing, and my favorite city to fly to is Lisbon. The people are so friendly, the weather is beautiful, there is so much to see, and, of course, the food and atmosphere are great. Flying to different parts of the world gives me the chance to learn about and interact with people of different cultures and to learn about the history of other places and the locals' way of life.

Despite the great opportunities of this career and seeing the world, every time I return to Canada I feel grateful to live in such an amazing country which has given a lot to me and my family. The opportunity to be based in my home country is tremendous.

CHAPTER 11

✈

MY MEMORABLE FLIGHTS

After twenty-one years of flying, I am still very excited every time I put on my pilot uniform and head to work to go fly an airplane. Every flight is special, and the ones where I have a close family member on board bring me great memories.

I had the opportunity to take my mom with me to Barcelona on her sixty-fifth birthday, where I had a forty-eight-hour layover. We were able to celebrate her birthday with the crew I was on that pairing with. Also, since my mom is a world traveler, I had the opportunity to take her with me on many flights I operated to Rome, where she left on cruise ships from the Port of Civitavecchia. It is a unique feeling when you know that your mom is sitting in the cabin and you are the captain of her flight. I know how proud she feels every time she's on my flights.

I also had the opportunity to fly my sister to Florida on the B737 when she was heading on vacation.

Malaga, Spain.

My little niece and I

What is also incredibly special is when kids and their parents visit the flight deck after a flight. I love to see their faces light up when they see all the switches and buttons in the cockpit; it reminds me of when I first walked in the cockpit as a kid.

I always enjoy chatting with our passengers. One question often asked by visitors is if we know what every switch in the cockpit is supposed to do. Another frequently asked question is what we do during all those hours. Many are surprised that such a big airplane like the A330 has a relatively small cockpit. They are also shocked by the size of the front windshield—some wonder how we get to see through it.

Other memorable flights were the ferry flights to and from Rio de Janeiro, Brazil, where we would fly our A330s for heavy maintenance inspections and overhaul. These were some of my favorite flights since Rio is a beautiful and magical place to visit. The descent and approach into Galeão International Airport (IATA: GIG, ICAO: SBGL) is always a fun experience, especially during the day; the view from the air is magical.

Sugarloaf Mountain, Brazil May 2019.

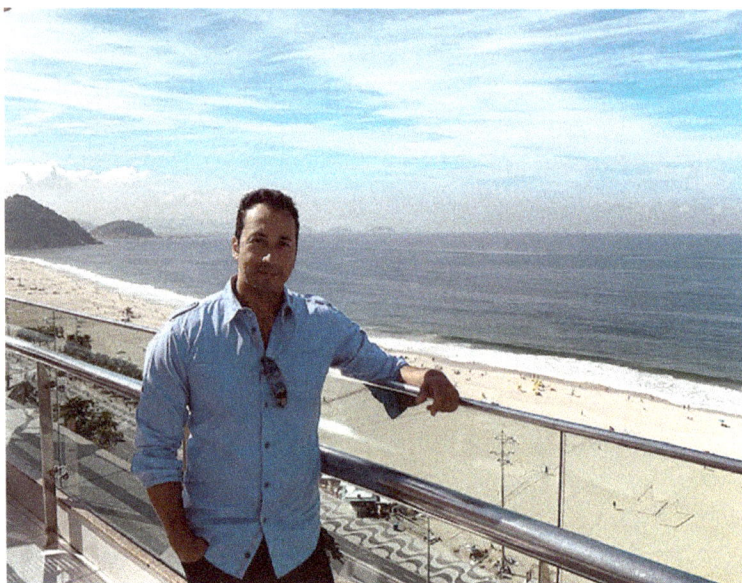

Copacabana beach, Brazil June 2019

Overflying the Amazon Rainforest, en route from Rio de Janeiro to Montreal, at 40,000 feet.

I once operated a flight to Hamburg, Germany on the A310; during the cruise portion the FD told us there was a Canadian rock band on board. When I asked her the name of the band, I could not believe it when she said it was the band The Tea Party.

The Tea Party is one of my favorite bands for a very long time, and I've seen them in concerts in Winnipeg and Toronto many times. I asked the FD to see if Jeff Martin, the band's lead singer, would be able to visit the flight deck after the flight, since I am a huge fan. I had a chance to speak with Jeff for a few minutes after the flight, who took the time to see us in the flight deck. Awesome!

THE BAND RUSH

The first time I listened to the band Rush was on CHOM FM 97.7 radio station in Montreal when I was around fifteen or sixteen years old. I became hooked on their music. The music and sound touch my soul. The science fiction and fantasy style music felt like it related somehow to flying. Listening to Rush gave me hope and motivation through the good and the challenging times in my aviation debuts and career.

My little brother and I were able to watch many of the band's live shows in Toronto, Montreal, and—one of our favorite shows—Las Vegas. We also had the opportunity to meet Geddy Lee during his "Book of Bass" signing in 2019. The song "Subdivisions" is one of my favorite Rush songs.

Sometimes when someone is trying to achieve a goal or a dream, we require some kind of a motivational push. For me, it was music and the band Rush.

Book signing with Geddy Lee, June 4, 2019.

WHEN AIRPLANES STOPPED FLYING—
THE INDUSTRY IS RECOVERING

The airline industry is unique in that it is often sensitive to what state the world is in. It is an industry that gets affected immediately when something happens in the world and takes the longest to return to normality and profitability.

The industry has gone through ups and downs during my twenty-plus-year career. The industry is sensitive to many situations in the world, such as the economy, the American dollar, oil prices, environmental issues (such as volcanic eruptions), terrorist threats and acts, wars, air disasters, high fixed and variable costs (such as airplane leases), political instabilities, airline reconstruction, airline merges, and much more. Bottom line, making a profit for airlines is very difficult.

I graduated from flight school in the late nineties and that was a difficult time to find any flying opportunities. The tragedy of the 9/11 attacks happened in 2001, and I was lucky to remain employed while many other pilots went through layoffs and company bankruptcies. It took a few years for the airlines to recuperate and for the public to have confidence in the safety of the industry. That was the first time I realized my profession is always at risk, not only in my part to be safe and not to make any mistakes on the job, but also in how the global situation could affect my job.

After 9/11 was the bird flu, the SARS outbreak, and volcano eruptions, just to name a few more events that disturbed airlines operations and profitability. Somehow I was lucky enough to not get laid off during those difficult times.

The year 2019 had been a remarkably busy and successful period for many airlines in Canada and around the world. My airline and many others were running ground schools and performing pilot interviews almost every month. Some airlines had to go on roadshows to promote and attract pilot applicants, which I took part in as well. It had been a long time since pilots in Canada could choose the major airline they wanted to pursue. As far as I could remember, pilots had always applied to a few airlines and accepted the first one that would offer employment, even if that airline wasn't their first choice. The goal was to get in and get that seniority number, but 2019 was completely different. That year was one of the best for pilots.

Then in 2020 everything changed. Initially when the news started to report about COVID-19 cases, I wasn't too alarmed and thought it was just an isolated event that would be dealt with very quickly. With the technology we have, I figured this situation would be contained fast and efficiently, and we would return to normal quickly. I am sure I wasn't the only one who thought this way.

Then as the weeks went by and the news was getting scarier, I started fearing that things were getting worse quickly. The change in the behavior of passengers during the COVID-19 crisis, travel restrictions, and the ensuing economic crisis had resulted in a dramatic drop in demand for airline services; by the end of April 2020, passenger travel dropped by 90%.

Many airlines started to park airplanes in various places around the world due to the travel demand becoming almost nonexistent. In over twenty years of flying, I had never experienced something so sad and alarming. I'd been lucky to remain employed all these years, but I now wondered what the future would hold for so many of us.

On April 1, 2020, I flew A330 C-GKTS aircraft from YYZ to YUL airport and then ferried C-GTSD A330 from YUL to YMX airport to park the airplane there for an undetermined time.

That day, walking in the Toronto Pearson and Montreal International airports, I was shocked to see how empty the terminals were. There were no passengers anywhere. All the airport kiosks and shops were closed. We are talking about Pearson airport here. It felt as if I was in a horror movie. *How did we get to this?* I asked myself. *When would things get back to normal?*

Every time I go flying, I remind myself of how lucky I am to do this line of work and enjoy every flight. As I taxied and lined up the Airbus

A330, on Runway 06R at YUL airport, that April 1, I felt that this might just be the last time I was going to fly, that maybe the airlines would never recuperate from this, that I may never work again as a pilot, and maybe people would not travel again for many years. All those thoughts went through my mind.

I savored the magnificent sound of the engines as they were spooling up for takeoff. The flight to YMX was short, and I mostly hand flew and did not use the autopilot.

As we landed in Mirabel, I could see the lineup of airplanes parked on one of the runways. That was the first time I had seen so many airplanes parked, and it hit me this was the real thing. Airlines parking their airplanes is a sign that things are not going very well.

Mirabel Airport, April 1, 2020.

Not long after that flight, the airline I was working with sent layoff notices to all the pilots and flight attendants. It was the first time in twenty-one years as an airline pilot that I was laid off. The layoff notice made me very sad and worried. The fact that I would not have an income for who knows how long kept me up some nights. But with this notice it was also a stop from flying—and that was hard to accept.

I started working at the age of thirteen, delivering newspapers, and never stopped working since and it had been thirty-two years.

The first day of layoff, I woke up not sure of what I was supposed to do. For the last six and a half years, I had a busy schedule as a supervisor: early mornings heading to the airline's HQ and giving ground courses, simulator flight tests, numerous meetings, and, of course, overseas flying. I guess this was what retirement feels like.

Like so many pilots worldwide, we were stuck in this unfortunate situation, some with families, kids, bills, and mortgages to keep up with. I could imagine the stress they had felt with this crisis.

To keep myself busy, I figured I'd work on my résumé and see if I could find any work, preferably flying opportunities, in the meantime until my airline started operations again. The problem was that as I was working on my résumé, 100% of my work experience for the last twenty years was flying as a pilot. All the jobs I was applying to required specific skills and experience that I didn't have. I did have management experience, but again, all of that was aviation related. I had heard some of my colleagues began driving long haul trucks and buses while others worked in vaccine clinics. These highly skilled professionals had to find work in any field they could.

I printed a bunch of résumés and returned to the international airport, just like I did twenty-two years ago, and handed out my résumé to any company whose door I could knock on. Although many airlines prefer online applications, as they do not want to have people walk into their offices, just like in 1999 I walked into the airlines headquarters and left my résumé with the receptionist or asked to see the chief pilot. The biggest difference now was that I had over 13,000 hours of flight experience and wasn't the only one with that experience. There were many other pilots trying to find any flying opportunities they could.

I sat in my car between résumé deliveries, wondering how we got into this situation. Not long ago I had been flying to Paris twice a month, and now I did not even know when I would be able to fly again.

That was when I decided that while I searched for work, I would also start writing a book about my journey in aviation, which was something I wanted to do for a long time but never could because I had been so busy with work all these years.

I needed to stay focused, challenge myself, and have a goal. I had to do something in my field, and writing a book about aviation—how it started for me and my journey to this present point—made sense. Even though no one was calling me for any flying jobs, I had a goal and a mission. With thousands of highly qualified pilots applying to the very few flying opportunities out there, I needed another approach and writing was the solution.

With the government restrictions, travel bans, and closure of many commercial buildings such as fitness centers, I found myself, as many others, restricted from the many activities I was used to doing before COVID started.

I scheduled my writing to four days a week, averaging three to five hours per day. This kept my morale up and kept me away from watching the news.

On June 17, 2020, I received a call from the A330 chief pilot informing me that I would be recalled back to work in mid-July. I listened a few times to the voicemail he had left me, I was just so happy with the news and to hear his voice again. Since I was twenty-fourth away from the last recalled pilot, the position I was able to hold was an FO, but I could still keep my check pilot credentials. I considered myself lucky since many of my colleagues were not recalled.

To requalify back on the airplane, I did my simulator requalification as a captain at the end of August and the line check with a fellow FO and the check pilot on the jumpseat on October 14 during a flight from Montreal to Port au Prince, Haiti, and back to Montreal. It felt great to be back in the cockpit, and although it had been a few months since my last flight, I felt right at home.

The airline had good intentions to restart the operations in the summer of 2020 despite no improvement in the COVID situation. The travel restrictions became worse and worse, and my airline was forced to stop operations again. I received my second layoff notice on October 19, 2020.

It was hard to accept the second layoff notice. I was hoping things would be improving instead of getting worse. I had to stay optimistic and not get discouraged, although some days were harder than others. I tried to stay fit despite the fact gyms were closed; I made myself a training routine and worked out at home. My writing breaks would be spent alone on the ice rink, keeping my skating skills sharp, with hopes that we would be allowed to play hockey again.

A big lesson I learned from this unfortunate situation was that pilots need a backup plan for their careers. Pilots spend countless hours advancing in their careers, but one should take the time to learn or study a backup field. It doesn't have to be a major career, just something to fall on in case the aviation industry comes to a halt just as history proves it has many times. With today's technology, we can join university courses remotely on our personal devices, which is something many should take advantage of.

In the airline industry, time goes by very fast. We bid the next schedule, and once it comes out we are busy with the flying and being away from home on the road. I've been flying for my airline for fifteen years, and I can remember the first day I started as if it was yesterday. Remember that time goes by fast in the airline industry, therefore you should use your free time wisely.

A few pilots I know were able to fall on their computer programing skills, accounting, or teaching side jobs. Find the time in your flying to study another trait, language, or skill. It will come in handy when you least expect it.

I was very fortunate to receive a phone call one day from a close friend who is also a Centre Leader at CAE Montreal Training Center. CAE is a global leader in worldwide training, producing more pilots across the globe than any other provider. Bob needed an instructor to perform some training sessions and simulator quality flyouts, an opportunity I happily accepted. I am very grateful towards CAE, as are many of my colleagues, for giving us that teaching opportunity when we were out of work.

A330 flight simulator, CAE Montreal, January 2022.

Mr. Robert Nag and I, CAE Training Center Montreal, March 2022.

I received my second recall notice and returned to flying duties as an FO on August 16, 2021 and had the opportunity to fly the Airbus A321 NEO. A few months later, I regained my captain and Type-rating Examiner position. I really enjoyed flying the state-of-the-art A321 NEO and was eventually transferred back onto the Airbus A330.

As I am writing this chapter, the aviation industry hasn't returned to normality or the productivity of 2019. But looking at history, the need for air travel, the eventuality of pilot shortage, and the industry recovery, I strongly believe that aviation will someday return to its full force and even reach record profitability.

Many airlines have already increased flight frequencies, more pilots' recalls have begun, and some airlines have even resumed pilot hiring.

If your dream is to pursue a career in aviation and to become a pilot, or just to get your pilot license, do not hesitate one second—no matter what state the aviation industry is in. I've been flying for twenty-five years now, and I am still excited to go flying before every flight. I'm proud to put on my uniform and grateful for the opportunity to do something I love and work with wonderful people. Flying has been a large part of my life, and it has been one of the greatest things that happened to me. It will also be for you as well! Thank you and all the best!

AFTERWORD

I have written some short essays in the past but never a book nor an autobiography. This project started a couple years ago, with about ten pages full of notes, events, and dates about my journey to becoming an airline pilot. There are many subjects I decided to keep out, as I thought they might not be interesting or relevant to this book, such as personal relationships.

My goal was to share the path that I took to achieving something I'd always dreamed of doing and what it took to get there. I also wanted to share what I've learned as a pilot by writing about my experiences. I believe every single pilot has their own special, amazing story and their own unique path to making their dream come true. Each pilot has had to make many sacrifices and work hard to make it in this very competitive industry. I hope my story will motivate anyone that is passionate about achieving a goal or making their dreams come true. There is no real secret formula. One needs to have a goal, work hard, and never give up. By staying positive, hungry to succeed, and humble, with a little luck great things will come true.

For me, there were many obstacles and challenges along the way, but looking back today, I'm glad they were there to push me even further and harder to achieve my goal and make my dream come true. It's all about progress!

"*One truth I have discovered for sure: When you believe that all things are possible and you are willing to work hard to accomplish your goals, you can achieve the next 'impossible' dream. No dream is too high!*"

— *Buzz Aldrin, American astronaut and fighter pilot*

ACKNOWLEDGMENTS

I am forever grateful for my family. Thank you to Mom, Catherine, and Nir for making all this come true. I could not have made it to where I am today if not for your love, support, and guidance.

Mark Killen, thank you for letting me bug you for seven months until you hired me and gave me that first shot in aviation, for being there for me during the ups and downs in life, and for your friendship.

Ron Adolph, thank you for all the knowledge and experience you shared with me, for letting me assist you in the training department, and for your friendship.

Robert Nag, thank you for everything you have done for me throughout the years, your trust, and your friendship.

Thank you for everyone involved with this book project. My book publishing team at FriesenPress who dedicated great time and effort with the book editing, planning, and design. My photographer Claude who worked tirelessly to get the great shots.

Thank you Carolanne for your support and encouragement.

To all the amazing people I got to work with throughout my career, who had confidence in me working beside them and letting me use my knowledge, experience, and skills.

To all my friends, thank you.

Finally, I am thankful to Air Transat and Perimeter's management for all the wonderful opportunities you have provided me through the years. Also, to the airlines and the industry that gave me opportunities, employment, and wonderful experiences.

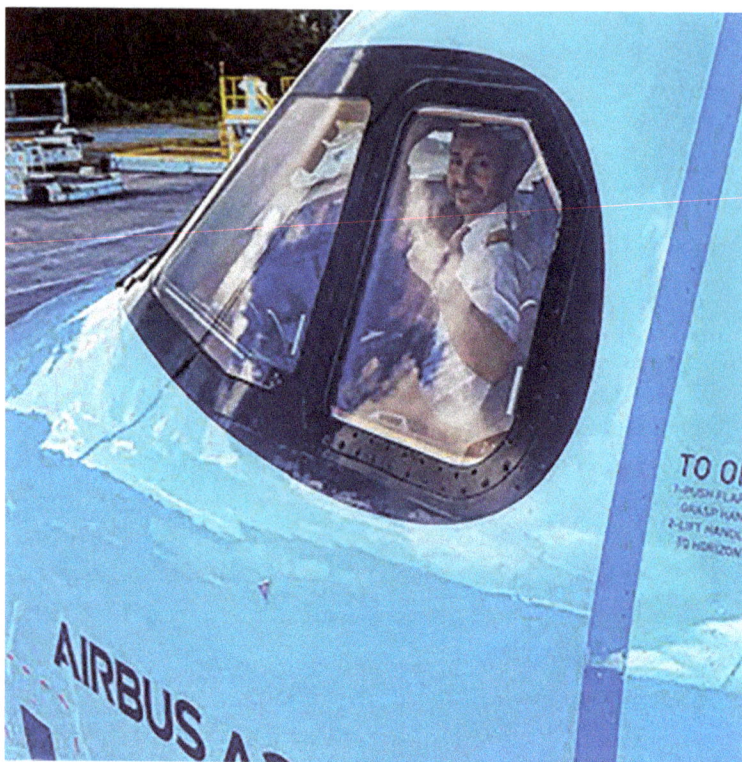

Photo Credits
Photos on pages 71, 75 and 76 courtesy of Ronen Raz
Photo on page 203 courtesy of Marc-André Lapierre

All other photos courtesy of Gerard Mofet

END

GLOSSARY

A, B, C, D

- Advanced Visual Docking Guidance System (A-VDGS)
- Airline Transport Pilot License (ATPL)
- Air Traffic Control (ATC)
- Amsterdam Schiphol Airport (AMS)
- Area Navigation (RNAV)
- Audio Control Panel (ACP)
- Auxiliary Power Unit (APU)
- Berens River Airport (YBV)
- Boeing B737 800 Next Generation (NG)
- Bombardier Canadair Regional Jet (CRJ)
- Collège Enseignement Supérieur de Pilotes d'Aéronefs (CESPA)
- Commercial Pilot License (CPL)
- Control Display Unit (CDU)
- Controlled Flight into Terrain (CFIT)
- Controller Direct Pilot Communication (CDPLC)
- Crew Resource Management (CRM)
- Decision Altitude (DA)
- Decision Speed (V1)

E, F, G, H

- Edmonton Airport (YEG)

- Electronic Centralized Aircraft Monitoring (ECAM)
- Exhaust Gas Temperature (EGT)
- Extended-Range Twin-Engine Operations (ETOPS)
- Evidence-Based Training (EBT)
- Fargo, North Dakota Airport (KFAR)
- Flight Crew Operating Manual (FCOM)
- First Officer (FO)
- Flight Management System (FMS)
- Flight Operations Department (Flight Ops)
- God's River Airport (ZGI)
- Global Positioning System (GPS)
- Heathrow Airport (LHR)
- High Frequency (HF)

I, J, K, L

- Inertial Navigation System (INS)
- Initial Approach Fix (IAF)
- Instrument Flight Rules (IFR)
- Instrument Landing System (ILS)
- Island Lake Airport (YIV)
- LaGuardia Airport (LGA)
- London Gatwick Airport (LGW)

M, N, O, P

- Minimum Equipment List (MEL)
- Minimum Descent Altitude (MDA)
- Montreal International Airport (YUL)
- Navigation Display (ND)
- Never Exceed Speed (VNE)
- Non-Directional Beacon (NDB)
- Non-Precision Approach (NPA)
- North Atlantic Tracks (NAT)
- Norway House Airport (YNE)

- Notice to Airmen (NOTAMS)
- Oxford House Airport (YOH)
- Pilot Flying (PF)
- Pilot-In-Command (PIC)
- Pilot Monitoring (PM)
- Pilot Not Flying (PNF)
- Pilot Proficiency Check (PPC)
- Private Pilot License (PPL)
- Puerto Vallarta Airport (PVR)

Q, R, S, T

- Quick Reference Handbook (QRH)
- Royal Canadian Mounted Police (RCMP)
- Red Sucker Lake Airport (YRS)
- Receiver Autonomous Integrity Monitoring (RAIM)
- Reference Landing Speed (VREF)
- Rotation Speed (VR)
- Saint-Hubert Airport (YHU)
- Stalling speed or the minimum steady flight speed in the landing configuration (VS0)
- Standard Instrument Departure (SID)
- Standard Operating Procedures (SOPs)
- Standard Terminal Arrival (STAR)
- St. Andrews Airport (YAV)
- St. Theresa Point Airport (YST)
- Takeoff/Go-Around Thrust (TOGA)
- Ted Stevens Anchorage International Airport (PANC)
- Thief River Falls Regional Airport (KTVF)
- Thompson Airport (YTH)
- Toronto Island Airport (YTZ)
- Toronto Pearson International Airport (YYZ)
- Traffic Alert and Collision Avoidance System (TCAS)
- Type-Rated Examiner (TRE)

U, V, W, X, Y, Z

- Vertical Navigation (VNAV)
- Very High-Frequency Omni-Directional Range (VOR)
- Visual Flying Rules (VFR)
- Visual Meteorological Conditions (VMC)
- Winnipeg International Airport (YWG)

.

Printed in the USA
CPSIA information can be obtained
at www.ICGtesting.com
LVHW061936151123
764029LV00012B/211